OUR
HIGHEST

MARY WILEY

OUR HIGHEST

90 DAYS OF KNOWING
AND LOVING GOD

A Theology Every Day Devotional

B&H
PUBLISHING
BRENTWOOD, TENNESSEE

For Caleb, Nora Kate, and Addie:
May the Spirit forever be cultivating an unquenchable hunger for God and His Word in you. He loves you so! I pray you grow up knowing and loving Him all of your days. In Him alone is truly abundant life. He is your highest good.

Love,
Mom

ACKNOWLEDGMENTS

The work of writing is a peculiar curiosity, demanding almost constant attention. If I'm not writing, I'm thinking about writing or talking about writing, and surprisingly to me, sometimes this fixation is unhelpful dinner conversation or vacation fodder. In any endeavor, especially such a consuming one as this, carving out time and space to do the work leaves caverns where other special moments might have been. John Wiley, you have never hesitated, not even once, to sacrifice on my behalf so that I might write or study. You've put me and this project first many times, and your support means the world. Thank you for the many times you told me to "go write or whatever it is you do." I literally could not do this without you! I love you!

Caleb, Nora Kate, and Addie, you have allowed me to be both mom and writer, with much grace for when Mom needed to be typing away at her computer when you'd rather me take you to the pool. This work is as much yours as it is mine.

To my mom, who let me pursue the most impractical degrees, knowing it could mean I ended up living in her basement (which would really be a turn of events because my childhood home doesn't have a basement). You have never hesitated to encourage. All the times I caught you with your Bible open in your lap as I grew up were instructive to me. I'm who I am today because of who you are.

To the many who have stoked my fire of greater understanding of God and His Word, thank you! This early love, sprouting at the careful tending of faithful Sunday school teachers and youth leaders has been pruned by teachers and professors, growing deep, lasting roots because you allowed the Spirit to use you. Thank you for serving and for answering my hundreds, if not thousands, of theological questions along the way.

What you hold in your hands has been a long time coming thanks to the wise ideation and patient prodding of Devin Maddox, who is boss, friend, and publisher. Thank you for believing in me and in this.

B&H team, I cannot express how much I love each of you! You are literally the best in the business, but far more than that, you love readers to Christ. Thank you for being my team, but also my friends, and in so many ways, my family. It is a joy to serve alongside you each day.

Reader, this is all for you. You've been loved before you knew this title existed. You've been prayed for long before now. Thank you for reading. May God move.

CONTENTS

The Attributes of God

INTRODUCTION

What you hold in your hands feels undone. In God's great kindness, I will know Him better tomorrow than I do today, and I will bitterly wish I could have included here what He reveals. Tomorrow, I will see Him more clearly. Tomorrow, I will experience His goodness more deeply. That is the gift of the Christian life, isn't it? The revealed beauty and majesty of God that we know today is just a shadow of all there is to know—all we will know—when we see Him face-to-face.

While these words feel undone, may we be the undone ones as we spend time lifting our feeble, finite eyes to God, who is infinite in glory. The clearer our vision of Him, the deeper our worship runs. There is no greater use of time or attention than to spend our days knowing and loving God. He has revealed to us all that is necessary for both, preparing the pursuit before us: theology. The word *theology* may bring back to you the smell of an old library, largely unvisited with musty decades-old carpet and dusty books, but the pursuit of theology, simply knowing and loving God, is far from this vision. God is so superior, so different, so other than all we see on earth. He cannot be explored like the other "ologies" that likely spike your cortisol levels just by their mention: biology, anthropology, psychology, geology. This is not a subject where pop quizzes abound.

Instead, theology is a relationship, a glorious meeting, an ongoing conversation with the God who created all things, including every detail tested on those pop quizzes. It is not cold and distant, but a working out of salvation that is full of vibrant life. Knowing our God who is infinitely good in all His essence and in all His ways is not simply an exercise of the mind.

True theology is communion with our God who is the source and definition of good, and learning to know that goodness as we love and worship Him. As Dorothy Sayers said, "the dogma [or the truth about God in all of His glory—theology] is the drama."[1] Theology isn't limp and lifeless. It is the glorious fullness of who God is and what He is doing, has done, and will do in the world. It's the best kind of drama, because the gospel is a dramatic rescue.

Theology drives your life, and whether you know it or not, you are already a theologian. From the minute you began asking questions about God as a little boy or little girl, even before you first believed, you were doing the work of theology. Every question, every curiosity, every process for making decisions is informed by what you believe is true about God and His world, and we want to be faithful in the way we think about Him and live in response..

That's our goal here: to do theology together every day so that we might not just be theologians, but good ones. This is not a simple intellectual exercise, but a whole-life kind of knowing, finding Him in the pages of Scripture and living a life congruent with the truths you find. This kind of knowing is beaming with abundant life for those who are seeking Him. Over the next 90 entries, we'll seek to know Him: His Person, His attributes, and His work in the world. This is what scholars call Theology Proper, or the study of the Triune God.

Each day is written to guide you to know and love God more deeply as you experience Him anew with a focus toward how this truth should also move you to worship, because the goal of theology is not to collect knowledge in our heads so that we might be the smartest in the room. The goal of right theology is always right worship: obedience in every aspect of our lives.

You and I are separated by time and space, but one in the body of Christ, journeying together on the narrow way. This is the narrow way that leads to life with God Himself as the prize. He has revealed Himself to us so that we might know Him and love Him, and my prayer has been that you seek and find Him in these pages with a fresh vision of His infinite goodness. He truly is good all the time: the highest good and our highest good.

Over the next 90 days, I pray these moments of knowing and loving Him sprout roots, growing deep into His Word. I'm asking God to wake you up early, to carve out time for you, and that He would give you the focus needed to spend time with Him before you touch your phone or stumble to retrieve your coffee only to be distracted by the dishes in the sink and the toys on the floor. If this is just a box to check off each day, a task on a to-do list, you won't stick with it for 90 days. It can't just be something you do; it has to be the necessary bread for your day, a gift from God to sustain you after you close its cover. It has to be someone you are becoming. I'm praying that you are different in 90 days—noticeably different—and that God uses these pages to cultivate life and joy deep in your bones, as a fan to flame. I'm also praying that He uses these pages as a scalpel, to cut away whatever is bent toward decay rather than life. May He humble you as you look upon His glory. May He empower you as you see clearly His grace. May He make you bold as you see clearly His power.

And as He does this, I pray that over and over again, you find Him to be better: better than the fascinations of your heart that lead you away from the source of Light and into the darkness. I don't know what particularly trips you up, but I know the One who cuts away the weeds from the path so that you stumble no more. I pray He gives you the sweet relief of walking smoothly as you journey with Him through these days. There is no better place to fix your eyes than upon the One who is more beautiful, glorious, and good than anything that livens your eyes on earth.

The cover of this book is full of growth and fruit, and I'm asking that God would do the same for you in your life—that He would make you a good tree, planted by His streams of water, and that even the most fruitful tree in the most productive orchard would look like famine compared to the fruit He brings in and through you.

I'm glad you are here. And I'm praying for you. May each entry drive you to your Bible, to your knees, and to action—good fruit.

God, please move.

OUR HIGHEST GOOD

You are good, and you do what is good;
teach me your statutes.
Psalm 119:68

"God is good . . . All the time. All the time . . . God is good." This is the call and response of our people, a battle cry of sorts. But do we truly believe it? Not just with our heads but with our hearts? I'm afraid we've become people who prefer the good that comes from God's hands but don't so much yearn for communion with the One who is good. It's easier to enjoy His riches than to consider His requirements—to marvel at His handiwork rather than at His holiness. Yes, His work is miraculous and wonderful, but the goodness of His work only flows through the goodness of the One who is doing that work.

God is good, not only when He is giving good to His people but also in the darkest night of the soul, the most painful of trials, and the mind-numbing monotony of days held in waiting. He is good when things are good with us, and when things are not. We stake our lives not on the works of His hands, but on the One whose hands do the work. He is the good life we seek.

Philosophers have sought to define humanity's highest good since the great thinkers began thinking. In Latin, the phrase is *summum bonum*, which literally translates as "the supreme good from which all others are derived."[2] Every school of thought has a recommended solution for finding the good life. Some recommend moral excellence, but we are incapable of it in our own strength. Others recommend beauty or rightness in itself, but without a rubric of sorts, both are judged by the eye of the beholder. It's not in human relations, because those often fail us, leaving no aroma of good in their wake. Neither can flourishing success or happiness bear the weight of defining good, because neither lasts forever. The quest for what lies at the top of the ladder on which all good things find their rung is not more of the same of what is below it. It is wholly other, Creator unlike His creation.

Yet, the One who is good has not left us to stumble blindly through life, hoping we find the path to the good life. Instead, God came near, revealing Himself in a way that we can understand: a piece of literature—His Word—and a man, the Word made flesh. It is in His Word—the Scriptures—that we can know and love Him, seeing His goodness from before He laid the foundations of the earth to today clearly in its pages. And it is in His Son that we may see the "radiance of God's glory and the exact expression of his nature, . . ." (Heb. 1:3).

If He is the highest good, then knowing and loving Him is our greatest good. We have been invited to participate in the divine life through the good work of the Son, the good plan of the Father, and the good gift of understanding through the Spirit. There is no greater way to spend our days than in preparing for eternity by knowing the One whom we will spend it worshipping. In His goodness, He knows us completely. There's no dark corner of our hearts left unturned. And still, He has invited us to know Him. The unknowable has made Himself known because He is good. The One to whom we could not ascend has descended to us. He truly is the highest good, and all His ways follow suit.

No one can do enough goal setting, habit hacking, networking, or working overtime to achieve the good life because the harder you strive, the more elusive it is. The good life isn't financial security, relational stability, health, or finding a way to do what you love and get paid for it. The good life is not found in a situation. It is found in a Person.

As the writer of Ecclesiastes finds chapter after chapter, there is no good if it is not God's good. There is no purpose if it is not God's purpose. Everything is vanities, a chasing after the wind. Everything is purposely monotony, spinning out of control in its unending resolutions, but with no intentionality or end. I have a dear friend who has refused to study Ecclesiastes with me for many years because in her words, "It's depressing." And it is. Because Jesus is the only right answer to the problem of Ecclesiastes. There is no good without God—and specifically, God made flesh: Jesus. But with Him, there is only good. He is the substance of good, its author. And all His ways are good because all His ways are love. His greatest good—and ours—is found in this: "No one has greater love than this: to lay down his life for his friends" (John 15:13).

Is He your highest good today? A day in His courts is truly better than one thousand elsewhere (Ps. 84:10). He is good. He is our highest good.

"God, and God alone, is man's highest good."[3]
—Herman Bavinck (1854–1921)

ADDITIONAL READING: 1 Chronicles 16:34; Romans 8:38–39

FROM WORD TO WORLD

In the beginning God created the heavens and the earth. Now the earth was formless and empty, darkness covered the surface of the watery depths, and the Spirit of God was hovering over the surface of the waters.
Genesis 1:1–2

In the beginning was the Word, and the Word was with God, and the Word was God. He was with God in the beginning. All things were created through him, and apart from him not one thing was created that has been created.
John 1:1–3

Cathedraled skies and the brightest stars, leafy sea dragons and spiny thistle; all things were made through the power of His Word, springing forth life with each ripple of sound. Words creating worlds. Our God speaks. His voice rings forth in the refrain of Genesis 1, "Let there be . . .", perfectly met each time with "And it was so" (Gen. 1:6–24). Who is this God who creates with no raw materials and paints the sky with no brush?

How might His immeasurable power be counted? What abundance of life must He hold that He would share it with both the whale and the fly?

He speaks, and out of nothing comes life. The Spirit hovers over the waters, near and intentional, preparing to cultivate life. An uninhabitable space became a flourishing place[4] as our triune God laid the foundations of the earth. Before units of measurement or the theories of physics, it was only God, holding perfect unity and communion within Himself, needing nothing. Yet the life within Him couldn't help but spill over, bringing life and light with His every word.

This bubbling over did not only testify to His creativity but was full of His infinite goodness. Of course, a well only gives that which is within, and a tree only bears its particular fruit. Everything God is and everything God does is good, because He *is* goodness. Like the warmth of the sun felt even through the window under the safety of a roof, His goodness emanates from Him, touching the entirety of creation and beyond. It is this goodness that is proclaimed as He raises His voice again at the end of each day, declaring His work good. This God who holds authority over all He made, declaring life or death in a breath, chose to actively extend His goodness to creation. His words don't only become worlds, but good worlds, glorious worlds. Worlds that point to the one-day story of a Savior who would die, but who would also live again.

This good work, done through the Son and for the Son (Col. 1:16), sings of His promise to enter the space and time He created—not as One separate from the creation He called good, but taking on flesh, becoming one with humanity. The One through whom all things were created would also dwell among us, redeeming us in His life, death, resurrection, and ascension. The turning of the seasons, the growth cycle of crops, the rising and setting of the sun all proclaim life from death, resurrection. Before time began, resurrection was on the mind of God. He is Creator, and He is also re-Creator.

However, this isn't just some Creator, as though He could be one of a number of gods. This is the One who created all in and through the Word. "In the beginning" doesn't just mean a moment in time, but according to Augustine, it also means in Christ, who is Alpha and Omega, beginning and end.[5] The only One who has power to create is also the One who has the power to enter that creation, taking on flesh: the Word. Creation comes through the Word. Life from death comes through the Word. The coming new creation comes through Him.

Our God speaks, and with His voice worlds are made. He is Creator. May we proclaim with Jeremiah the prophet: "Oh, Lord GOD! You yourself made the heavens and earth by your great power and with your outstretched arm. Nothing is too difficult for you!" (Jer. 32:17).

May His Word build His infinitely good kingdom in you as you learn to know and love Him, and may He do the same in the world through the work of your hands.

ADDITIONAL READING: Genesis 1–2; Jeremiah 32:17; Hebrews 3:4; Romans 1:20

HE MAKES HIMSELF KNOWN

*Long ago God spoke to our ancestors by the prophets at
different times and in different ways. In these last days,
he has spoken to us by his Son. God has appointed him
heir of all things and made the universe through him.*

Hebrews 1:1–2

A unique frustration comes with moving into a new neighborhood, starting a new job, or even going to your child's first game in a new season with a new team. It's mildly terrifying to me, really—the awkward silences and "What do you do?s." I want to skip pleasantries and go straight to deep relationships, but there are no shortcuts. Wired within our deepest needs lies an ache to be truly known and loved. Do you feel it? The gnawing to please, to be liked so that you might be known (at least the good and lovable pieces of you)? The hope that at least the good and lovable pieces might lead others to love you. We want to be known, but we also want to know: to know rightly and to know truly. And you likely hold this ache to truly and rightly know and be known by God too. But how do you get to know God who is not like you, who can't sit down across from you with a cup of coffee?

God is ontologically different from humanity, so the way we know Him must be different. And in His great goodness, He hasn't left this knowing up to us to do with some immense amount of intellect or effort. When we had no way to know Him, He made Himself known. When we could not ascend to Him, neither physically nor spiritually, He descended to us, taking on a language and method that we understand, so that we might know Him, and know Him sufficiently. He has done this in two ways: in His Word and in His Son, the Word made flesh (John 1:14). This is His special revelation. Jesus has come not only to fix our sin problem, but to fix our broken knowledge of God. He is not simply a mirror that shows us the reflection of God, a conduit of knowing about God but not like Him in substance. He is God, and we meet Him in the pages of Scripture.

Across three continents and more than two thousand years, the Spirit divinely inspired faithful servants to record His Word so that we may know Him. As church father Ambrose of Milan said, "He in holy Scripture walks in the hearts and minds of each and every one us."[6] Here, Ambrose was drawing a connection between the intimacy Adam and Eve had in the garden with the intimacy we have through His Word. We see His glory and His deliverance, His holiness and His rightful wrath, and while we do not walk in the same dirt Jesus did, we see Him in the pages of Scripture. We know Him as the Word of God—His Good News—in the Word of God. He didn't just show us the image of God; He *is* God, and He became as we are so we might be like Him.

When you could not know God on your own, He intervened. He came. He provided. He has spoken in a language we can understand and shown us the way to life, not just in His Words, but in the righteous life, death, resurrection, and ascension of Jesus.

He is a communicating God, communicating in the closed canon of His Word until He returns. He is not silent. We must simply listen. Read. Seek. Pray. May we know Him deeply, and not just as the Actor in the stories of old, but as the One who indwells us. Not simply as something that happened, but as Someone who is active and moving today. What does your time in His Word look like? How are you seeking to know Him deeply in the pages of His Word and the life of His Son?

ADDITIONAL READING: Matthew 11:27; 1 Corinthians 2:10–12; Colossians 1:15–20

BREATH OF LIFE

*Then the L*ORD *God formed the man out of the dust*
from the ground and breathed the breath of life into
his nostrils, and the man became a living being.
Genesis 2:7

Dust. God took what was seemingly the most insignificant substance and formed it into man. This is not even nutrient-rich, compost-soaked soil, hand-mixed for your fancy garden kind of dirt. It's dust. Useless, valueless dust. Shake it from your feet, sweep it from your floor. Dust.

Nothing was growing in it and it looked a lot more like death than life. Yet the One who brings life came near to it, forming man from this insignificant, valueless dust. Like a priceless van Gogh made of the same canvas and paints used for preschool finger painting, the Maker brings the value because He did the forming. Unlike the other creatures who breathe, God breathed His life into man, depositing eternity within. This is the pinnacle of God's creation: man and woman in the image and likeness of God, made to live forever with Him. The breath of the living God brought true life to Adam's dusty bones, and with it came God's likeness and image.

Life is more than a capacity to inhale and exhale. This is the breath of God that brings about the life-giving communion of man and God, and it is what is lost when Adam and Eve sin. From Adam's rib, Eve would be shaped: "bone of my bone and flesh of my flesh" (Gen. 2:23). God gave the gift of life, but also life with Him and life with one another. There was no other acceptable partner from among creation than another who carried the breath of life, the image of God.

Elsewhere in Scripture, God "raises up from dust" to a royal assignment, just as Adam is made from the dust of the ground and given an important role in ruling over God's creation (see 1 Sam. 2:8).[7] God gave Adam and Eve a purpose and good work to do, revealing Him in their cultivation of creation. Made from dust but given authority as God's representatives. Made from dust, but the home of His breath, lungs full of the goodness of God. Yet Adam and Eve were immature and unwise, disobeying God and trading in this life for death and suffering. Their disobedience would require they return to dust, and in their lives, they would be separated from the breath of God, looking more like God's other creatures than like God Himself because they would be lacking communion with Him.

Yet, God was not surprised. Before the foundation of the earth He planned a way for them to be returned to garden-like enjoyment of God through His Son, who would take on our dust-born flesh. Through Him, our dust-bound flesh can be renewed, life breathed into it again for today and all eternity, which will bring with it our resurrected bodies and uninterrupted communion with God. He gives life and sustains it, both today and forever. All He is and all He does stirs up life, as He is life's Source and Sustainer, its Author and Giver.

The breath we often take for granted today is borrowed. The true life that fills our lungs has never been our own. We are but dust, made alive through His breath. With every inhale and exhale, we proclaim His lordship, testifying to the goodness of a Maker who has not just shaped us, but shared His breath—His life—with us. As you breathe in, pray this: "Lord, You are good." As you breathe out, pray this: "And You alone sustain my life." Every breath is His anyway.

> Let everything that breathes praise the
> Lord. Hallelujah! (Ps. 150:6)

ADDITIONAL READING: Genesis 1:26; Job 33:4; Romans 6:4

5

WHAT'S IN A NAME?

God replied to Moses, "I AM WHO I AM. This is what you
are to say to the Israelites: I AM has sent me to you." God also
said to Moses, "Say this to the Israelites: The LORD, the God
of your ancestors, the God of Abraham, the God of Isaac, and
the God of Jacob, has sent me to you. This is my name forever;
this is how I am to be remembered in every generation."
Exodus 3:14–15

Mary—the beloved name of the mother of our Savior, the name my parents chose for me in the '80s when it was certainly waning in popularity, the name my now husband thought made me at least thirty years older than him when a friend told him about me for the first time—boasts a lovely meaning. I stumbled upon it in a baby book alongside my friends in the bookstore at a youth camp in high school. Among a Courtney and a Tiffany, I thought the meaning of my name would blow them all away. Instead, as I flipped to my name, the wind was knocked out of my pride's lungs. This name I received at birth by loving parents didn't mean joy or delight. It meant bitter. Bitter—what a legacy! Years later, with much relief, I learned that it also could mean beloved, and I've wondered many times if this baby book was single-handedly responsible for my name's waning popularity.

Names matter. Even before you can introduce yourself by it, your name becomes a primary marker of your identity. It's personal, separating those who know you from those who do not. As God met with Moses through a bush that was burning, but not burned up, He spoke of His personal name for the first time: Yahweh: "I AM."

The being verb here is *hayah* (or *ehyeh*), which Moses would quickly recall from the creation account. The repeated "and *there was* light" (Gen. 1:3) or sky (Gen. 1:6) or "And it was so" in some translations holds this same verb. Moses would have instantly known the God who brought forth life with His voice was the One calling to Him. His name testified to His nature and His work, and He was continuing it in this message for His prophet. The revelation of God's personal name was a declaration of His active presence[8] with Moses and, in turn, His presence with us. He is a self-revealing God, showing His people who He is and what He is like. He intervenes and seeks to be known: "I AM." He needs no object. He need not further explain Himself. He is. He always has been.

The Israelites cried out to God in their 430 years (Exod. 12:40) of crushing captivity and back-breaking striving in Egypt, and here is God's response: "I AM." "I AM" with you. "I AM" not unaware of your suffering. "I AM" the God who was—the God of Abraham, Isaac, and Jacob, and the God who is to come—the One to be remembered in every generation, the true, living God who hears and who acts. I AM.

This name is so holy that His people would not say it aloud, instead using Jehovah, meaning "the name," or Adonai, meaning Lord, and yet He spoke of His name to Moses so that he might know the One he was called to worship. He revealed Himself so that He might be the source of hope and comfort in affliction for the Israelites for the years to come. He intervened and drew near, doing something about the cries of His people. The self-existent, all-powerful, creation-speaking, omnipresent, aware, active, and infinitely good God drew near.

What do you face today that has you wondering if God hears your cries? If He'll ever respond? In the darkest of Israel's days, God showed up in fire, promising His presence. And in our darkest days, He always shows. He has entered into our crushing captivity and back-breaking striving, setting us free through the spotless sacrifice of Jesus on the cross for our sin.

This Jesus also said, "Truly I tell you, before Abraham was, I am" (John 8:58). I AM took on flesh and dwelt with His people, and then, in an act of ultimate nearness, the Father and Son sent the Spirit to dwell within His people. I AM, the God who made Himself known through a burning bush, has also revealed His all-encompassing power and goodness by revealing His name to His people. He is nearer than your thoughts—than the clothes upon your skin. We know His name. And He knows yours. Comfort abounds in Him.

ADDITIONAL READING: Isaiah 48:12–13; John 8:48–59

6

THERE IS NO ONE LIKE OUR GOD

"Listen, Israel: The LORD our God, the LORD is one."
Deuteronomy 6:4

Before there were people who could worship at His feet, God was worthy of all worship. Before the nations of the world were sown, He was perfectly sovereign over each one, charting their rise and fall. Nations would exalt their kings and their gods, and often their kings as gods, all while the true God, the only God, was at work. He doesn't need assistance from other "lesser gods." The true God is One. He is not one among a pantheon of gods as in Egypt, but He is superior over all because He is the only living God. There's no need for more.

The affirmation of God's complete otherness—His Oneness—is the reminder presented in Deuteronomy 6 to God's people who are settled in Moab on the east side of the Jordan. They are waiting to enter the Promised Land of Canaan, which is just across the water. Most of those Moses was speaking to had only heard about God's deliverance in Egypt, and they had been influenced by their parents and even grandparents who grew up under Egypt's gods. This is the group who would go into the Promised Land. The listeners had been born in the wilderness, and after the generation who disobeyed God passed away (including Moses), this group would go into the land. Deuteronomy records a second giving of the Law and a second emphasis on who God is so that those who were going into the land flowing with milk and honey would know and obey the God who gave it to them.

Canaan would be a land given and governed by God, not a king or pharaoh. The people were to worship this rightful Ruler, not the multitude of gods of Egypt or the other nations around Canaan because those gods hold as much power as the stone gnome in my neighbor's garden. They don't hear, move, or act. They have no power because they have no life. All of life is in the Lord, who is One. He is its source, and the source of all other good. His attributes are like a beautiful harmony, all infinitely active simultaneously and none in dissonance with one another. He cannot be divided from His nature or essence because He *is* those things: love, joy, peace, and more. This Oneness confirms that He can be trusted because He is unchanging, ever and always good. Ever and always kind. Ever and always powerful.

We often operate as if His Oneness is a fiction we pretend to believe, as if it was true in the Old Testament, but then we meet Jesus and learn there's actually three. Yet Jesus also confirms that there is only One God. Our God is Three Persons and One God. There is not a God behind Him that He came to tell us about, as if He is simply a messenger for someone greater. He *is* the One God, perfectly united in Father and Spirit as the Son. He is One with the Father (John 10:30), and it is the Spirit that He sends (16:7).

If He is One (and the only One), then He must be the self-giving Giver of life and the fully sufficient Provider for all of our needs. We don't need a multiplicity of deities to sustain the cosmos. It is this God who is One, supreme over all, that holds the universe in its place, commands the sun and the moon and the stars, gives and sustains life, and who is worthy of our undivided worship, for He is undivided, unconflicted, and always good. He is God . . . One.

His Oneness proclaims His capacity—His omnipotence, omniscience, and omnipresence. If He is One, then there can be no other. And if there can be no other like Him, then He must be every good thing, the Creator and Sustainer of all there is. His kingdom will never end. Our God is One. Do not fall to the lesser gods that do not hear or move. This is not just a necessary reminder for those crossing the Jordan. This is a necessary call to remember God who is One for us too.

Has your heart been captivated by the lesser gods that those around you worship? Has security, comfort, or the approval of others determined your steps and set a sort of law for your living? Have you created idols that you use as a sort of council of gods alongside the One true God? Return to Him. He needs no assistant. He is better. To know Him and to love Him is the greatest gift, the home of our purpose, and the source of all good. As God calls you out into deeper water with Him, may the depths teach you to trust and the brilliance of what you see leave you radically changed.

ADDITIONAL READING: Deuteronomy 6:4–9; Deuteronomy 11:13–21; Numbers 15:37–41; 1 Timothy 2:1–6

THE GLORY OF OUR TRIUNE GOD

For through him we both have access in one Spirit to the
Father. So, then, you are no longer foreigners and strangers,
but fellow citizens with the saints, and members of God's
household, built on the foundation of the apostles and
prophets, with Christ Jesus himself as the cornerstone.
Ephesians 2:18–20

The content of our faith is wholly dependent upon the object of our faith, and the good news is only good if God is triune. Without the distinctness of the Father, Son, and Spirit, then God taking on flesh as a baby in a manger would have left heaven empty and no Spirit of God working in the hearts and minds of those who would come to understand the good news of the gospel while Jesus was on earth. Without the Oneness of God, Jesus's blood was spilled without cause. What was required for the covering of sin would have been ineffective because if Jesus was not fully God, then He would not have been an acceptable holy, sinless, perfect sacrifice. Without both the simplicity and distinction of the Persons of God, then Jesus would not have risen from the dead, but God would be dead in a tomb, leaving us with no hope. But this is not the case, because Jesus was raised through the will of the Father and the power of the Spirit. He is not three-in-one as if there are three parts of a whole, and He's not three-or-one as if He can only be either/or. He is not even three-but-one as if those two truths were contradictory or negative. God is Three Persons *and* One God.

He is not like an egg with three parts able to be separated between egg, yolk, and shell. He is not like the phases of water, one element shifting between water, condensation, and ice dependent upon external circumstances to create these changes. He is not like one person who is simultaneously a wife, daughter, and friend. Every illustration falls apart under the weight of His uniqueness. Under the pressure of His glory, nothing on earth can compare. He is not a team of gods that are so close they always agree, but one God who has one will and one essence, and we have been invited to participate in this divine communion through the Son, in the Spirit, to the Father.

The math doesn't math, but we believe in faith what the Bible proclaims: God is three Persons and One God. My mind does not understand all the inner workings and I don't think it will on this side of seeing Him face-to-face, but I still rejoice in the goodness of God that Father, Son, and Spirit would share a will, with its pinnacle that we might know Him and love Him. He has chosen to reveal Himself to us through His Word and through His Word made flesh, Jesus. In John 14:9, Jesus says, "The one who has seen me has seen the Father." We know God because He has come near to us, not because we have somehow ascended to Him with profound understanding. And in this coming near, He has revealed Himself to us relationally: as Father, as Son, and as Spirit. Each Person is equally divine, sharing in all of His attributes with no hierarchy of power or status, and each Person is coeternal, uncreated and existing before there was time. They always act together—from the Father, through the Son, in the power of the Spirit. It is through the Son that we may commune with the Father, as He has made us right with Him, and it is in the Spirit that we are united into the body of

Christ. While the word *trinity* is not in the Bible, the concept is throughout (Gen. 1:1–2; Col. 1:16; Matt. 3:13–17; Matt. 28:19–20). We are in Him and He in us. We are able to commune with God because He is triune, as He acts as both Sovereign and Mediator, King and Priest.

Where our mental faculties fail us, our faith holds strong, filling in the gaps. The incomprehensible beauty of the Trinity is on display in the creed written in AD 325 in Nicaea. Spend time focusing on the One whom it proclaims and allow its truths to take root in your heart and mind. He is the object of our faith, our highest good.

> I believe in one God, the Father Almighty, Maker of heaven and earth, and of all things visible and invisible.
>
> And in one Lord Jesus Christ, the only-begotten Son of God, begotten of the Father before all worlds; God of God, Light of Light, very God of very God; begotten, not made, being of one substance with the Father, by whom all things were made.
>
> Who, for us men for our salvation, came down from heaven, and was incarnate by the Holy Spirit of the virgin Mary, and was made man; and was crucified also for us under Pontius Pilate; He suffered and was buried; and the third day He rose again, according to the Scriptures; and ascended into heaven, and sits on the right hand of the Father; and He shall come again, with glory, to judge the quick and the dead; whose kingdom shall have no end.[9]

ADDITIONAL READING: Isaiah 48:16; Galatians 4:6; 1 Corinthians 6:11; Romans 8:9

HIS KINGDOM WILL
HAVE NO END

"He will reign over the house of Jacob forever,
and his kingdom will have no end."
Luke 1:33

Now to the King eternal, immortal, invisible, the only
God, be honor and glory forever and ever. Amen.
1 Timothy 1:17

How many times a day do you think about the Roman Empire? A social media trend revealed that many men claim their minds wonder at the marvel of ancient Rome as many as three times a day, shocking their female counterparts.[10] And there's no shortage of marvels on which to think. Yet, what was the most successful empire the world has ever seen met a fate like many before and after it. Empires rise and fall, seeking unending control both in the boundaries of the empire and the time of its rule, but without success. Like ancient Rome, we want full control, but we can't have it. We are an empire-building people when we've been called to join God in His kingdom-building work. We want to be the sole captain of our lives, believing shipwreck is immanent if we aren't at the helm, when truthfully, it's never more immanent than when we take the wheel. Control is a mirage, after all. It's the light on the horizon that we're always chasing, but never reach.

Are you grasping for control today hoping maybe this time it will work? We so quickly forget our narrow vision and vaporous lives, believing our short years have taught us enough to build our own kingdom into something that will last, but it will not stand. Our empires are built of sticks and straw compared to the eternal kingdom of God and His good reign. Our empires topple at the lightest wind after a lifetime of unending sweat, full of hurry, striving, struggle, and frustration. Like Eve, we think we can manage what God manages, forgetting that He is eternal in all of His ways, perfectly wise and commanding every atom in the way it should go. If we had the amount of control we seek, it would crush even the most ambitious. This is why He is King and we are not.

He is not an earthly king whose death brings chaos for his kingdom with a transition of power. Instead, this King is One whose earthly death ushers in the reality of His reign. He is not an earthly king who changes his mind, who ignores the needs of his people, or who can't protect them. Instead, there's nothing that happens outside of our true King's intention, whether chaos or order, and His intentions for us are always good. He has always reigned, and He always will. We don't fear tomorrow because the same King reigns. We know His character, and it doesn't change. There's no threat of famine, exile, or captivity. His is a kingdom of flourishing, and it is eternal. The One who is I AM, who is before the mountains and before the world began, who is not just from eternity to eternity in the sense of time, is in every measurable good: love, peace, gentleness, patience, justice, and wisdom.

Let us spend our lives where it matters, in an eternal kingdom, one far greater than ourselves, rather than in a tiny empire painstakingly built brick-by-brick by our own hands. Let us bow to the King who is not only in control, but who is near, intimately involved in the daily lives of His people. He's a sacrificing King, pouring out His love in care for those who have no power of their own, allowing none of His people to perish under His care. He does not send His people into the worst battles, but fights for them, more powerful than the most cunning of enemies. He is King and He is good. And His kingdom will last forever.

Release your white-knuckled grip on what you think is the steering wheel of your life. It is but an illusion, unconnected to the vehicle and like a child's toy. Relax, for the eternal King is on His throne. Though chaos may swirl, you don't have to sort out every issue that is not yours to sort. God has gifted us the ability to be citizens of His kingdom, without the responsibility of being its kings. He is the good King we don't always want, but most certainly need. You are not in control. Instead, you are free to live as a child of the King. You are free to rest because He doesn't. Let go. The world will keep spinning because the One who spins it is on the throne.

ADDITIONAL READING: Psalm 90:2; Jeremiah 10:10a; Hebrews 1:1–12; Revelation 19:11–16

9

COVENANT MAKER AND KEEPER

"Instead, this is the covenant I will make with the house
of Israel after those days"—the LORD's declaration. "I will
put my teaching within them and write it on their hearts.
I will be their God, and they will be my people."
Jeremiah 31:33

I wear a ring on my finger, a circle purified and forged in fire. Despite its beauty, this symbol of the marriage covenant doesn't hold its substance. Vows spoken under the accountability of God testify to the promise, but they are not the primary law that governs a marriage. The promises of marriage—the conditions of the covenant—are found in the vows. What holds man and wife to their vows is not duty, but love: a promise of heart must be stronger than the simple repeat-after-me's.

The covenants between nations in the ancient Near East were normally wholly duty, held to the letter of the law rather than its heart. Following the Suzerain treaty model, a stronger nation would agree to provide protection and land in exchange for their loyalty, testified by the covenant sealed by blood as in Genesis 15.[11] The blood shed by animals testified the appropriate payment if the covenant was not kept: death. This was the model of the Old Covenant, leading to sacrifices made in the tabernacle or temple due to the disobedience of God's people to the given Law, but God's Law was never wholly duty. God was never after begrudging obedience; not with Abraham or Isaac or Jacob, and not with Moses or the people of Israel. He was always after the hearts of His people, not that they would obey for obedience's sake, but that they would obey for love's sake. He would protect and provide a land, and while there would be seasons of discipline, there was never a time that God broke His side of His covenant promises. Not to Adam, not to Abraham, not to Noah, not to David, and not to us.

Even better than the ones before, Jeremiah 31:33 speaks of a New Covenant not through the blood of animals or the blood of circumcision (the sign for the Old Covenant), but a covenant sealed by the blood of Jesus. This covenant would not be written on stone tablets that break or scrolls that deteriorate, but on the hearts of His people. God, the good covenant-maker, would also be the covenant-keeper, making a way for us to be made right not through our sacrifices or our own righteousness, but through His. His blood was poured out as a seal of the promise. We were hopelessly lost in our sin, deserving of no good thing under past covenants which we were incapable of fulfilling. And even so, He rescued us out of that need by providing Jesus as the perfect sacrifice—His body broken for us and His blood poured out—and He will keep this covenant into eternity, protecting and securing us in His presence and preparing a land—an eternal home—for us.

When we are faithless, doing whatever seems right in our own eyes (like in Judges 21:25), He remains faithful. He didn't only keep His covenants, but He also pursued us, establishing them. No matter what you face today, rest in His faithfulness. What He promises, He will do. He is and will be corporately faithful to His people—and He is and will be individually faithful to you. Are you resting in His covenant of grace, written on your heart, that has been sealed by the blood of Jesus? Both in your failure and success and your rebellion and obedience, God will continue to pursue you. No disobedience and no dishonor can remove His good promises kept for you in Christ Jesus.

ADDITIONAL READING: Zechariah 9:11; Matthew 26:28; 2 Corinthians 1:20; Hebrews 9:11–15; Hebrews 13:20–21

A BLESSING TO THE NATIONS

The LORD said to Abram:
"Go from your land,
your relatives,
and your father's house
to the land that I will show you.
I will make you into a great nation,
I will bless you,
I will make your name great,
and you will be a blessing.
I will bless those who bless you,
I will curse anyone who treats you with contempt,
and all the peoples on earth
will be blessed through you."
Genesis 12:1–3

"Go, therefore, and make disciples of all nations, baptizing them
in the name of the Father and of the Son and of the Holy Spirit,
teaching them to observe everything I have commanded you.
And remember, I am with you always, to the end of the age."
Matthew 28:19–20

Somewhere around 2004, I boarded the first of three planes, ranging from jumbo jet to tiny puddle jumper between my hometown and Nicaragua. As a kid who couldn't even drive yet, I saw the heart of God in the eyes of those who came to the community health clinics and kids' clubs our team staffed. It was here that I got a taste of God as a sending God for the first time as He allowed us to join Him in His great mission. In a moment, my life would never be the same. I saw His love for the nations and His call to us to go so that all might know Him, so that heaven may be full of the worship of every people, tribe, and tongue.

In Genesis 12, God calls Abram to leave all he knew in the pagan land of Ur to go into a new land. Abram has no map, no time line, and no promise that he wouldn't face extreme hardship. Every step would be entirely reliant upon the God who was sending him. Yet still, he goes. He responds to the first of many missionary calls recorded in the pages of Scripture to go and be a blessing. This is the call of every Christ-follower and is ultimately seen in the sending out of Christ who left heaven so that He might be a blessing to every person who would ever place their feet in the dirt of this earth. This dirt is compacted along the path by the many feet that went before us, joining in God's call to join Him where He is working. To go, to tell, to bless, and to baptize, not as a result of your striving or your genius evangelism strategy, but because of the One who sends—the One who is doing the blessing and who is with you always, even to the end of the age. While God may call us to cross the boundary lines of nations or languages, it is He who moved beyond every border that separated us from God. God is so different in His being that we could not understand or be right with Him on our own. So, when we couldn't help ourselves, He took on flesh, becoming like us, so that we might understand. He is the solution to both our broken communion with God and our broken understanding of Him. He entered our broken culture of darkness in flesh so that we may see Him clearly, but also so that His light may invade every dark space, setting on fire a light within us so that this light may cover the earth—every dark spot made light, every dead spot made alive.

Our God is a sending God. His love is so expansive, so infinite, that it cannot be held in our singular hearts or our singular homes. True light cannot be hidden. Our feet can't help but tread upon the path of His faithfulness. True obedience does not sit still for long. God is working. He is a sending, missional God. He has blessed all the people on earth through the Savior He sent, through the lineage of Abraham, Isaac, and Jacob, and allowed us to join Him in the continual blessing as those who are both united in Christ and empowered to share the good news of Jesus with a dark world. Be the light.

He sends families into far-off, unknown lands to be light in dark places, prophets into lands that are not their own to kings that they do not know to deliver both judgment and joy, the apostles out at the birth of the church to take the gospel into the surrounding nations and beyond by the power of the Holy Spirit.

Where is He calling you to go? Where might you make His name great? The question is not if you are called; the question is where? Is it to your home? Your neighborhood? Your workplace? The coffee shop you visit each week? The people far away from you and far away from God? He is a sending God. He sent His Son and He even orchestrated those who would share His good news with you. Not *if*, but *where*. So where is it for you?

ADDITIONAL READING: Exodus 19:5–6; Acts 1:8; 1 Peter 2:9–10

TRUE FREEDOM THROUGH THE TRUE DELIVERER

Then God spoke all these words: I am the LORD your
God, who brought you out of the land of Egypt, out of the
place of slavery. Do not have other gods besides me.
Exodus 20:1–3

For we know that our old self was crucified with him so
that the body ruled by sin might be rendered powerless so
that we may no longer be enslaved to sin, since a person
who has died is freed from sin. Now if we died with
Christ, we believe that we will also live with him.
Romans 6:6–8

As a teenager, I wanted one thing: freedom. But the kind of freedom I desired was the last thing I needed. What if freedom isn't a lack of boundaries, but like living within the protective walls of a good city, like being delivered from slavery to a better authority? The search for the Western view of "freedom" is a fruitless search for control without a capacity for it. Freedom from every oversight for both the kind and the hateful is a terrifying thought—anarchy even—far from the good, orderly kingdom of God where true freedom is abundant life that flourishes within the confines of His good instructions.

Our God is an intervening Deliverer, rescuing His people from sure death before King Ahasuerus through Esther (Esther 7–8), David from Saul's murderous intention (2 Sam. 22), and Ruth from her circumstances through Boaz, the Kinsmen Redeemer (Ruth 4). One of the most dramatic deliverances in human history occurs in Exodus, as God leads His people out of Egypt. This is the context of Exodus 20:1–3. God is preparing to give them the Law, but not without reminding them of the character of who it is they serve. This is the *why* of their obedience. God delivered them out of slavery.

We rightly hate slavery, looking back with great disdain that people would choose to be overlords of other humans who are created in the image of God and valuable to Him. We think of ourselves as anything but captives, but this is how Scripture describes our spiritual condition before we submit to Jesus. We are enslaved to the overlord of sin, with death and destruction as its foremen. The backbreaking work of Israel in Egypt looks like paradise in comparison.

God's people were not set free from slavery in Egypt simply to inherit a new slavery under this new Law. It was the path to true freedom. The Enemy will convince you that you need no rules or boundaries, that true freedom is found in doing whatever you want because independence is the ultimate good. Life is short; live it up. And yet, this is like begging to go back to Egypt, the land of enslavement.

God hasn't only delivered us from our slavery to sin. He has also rescued us from ourselves and our own self-destructive tendencies, inherited by Adam. We don't always recognize freedom when we see it. Instead, destruction looks seductive, pleasing to the eye and to be consumed. But "after desire has conceived, it gives birth to sin, and when sin is fully grown, it gives birth to death" (James 1:15).

God has orchestrated salvation to save us from this death, rescuing us from the infectious claws of sin and delivering us *to* something—to Someone. Freedom from sin actually comes by way of death, from the only One who has passed through it victoriously. Jesus has triumphed over sin on your behalf. If you are in Christ, you are dead to sin (Rom. 6:5–6), no longer dragging it as a heavy chain. You have been resurrected with Christ. The living don't spend their time among the catacombs, and the free don't spend their time putting back on their chains.

You've been miraculously freed. While habits of sin can be overwhelming, God has given you Himself and His people to hold you in deliverance. Call a friend. Plan a meeting time. Bring your sin into the light so you can look down and see the chains around your wrists have no lock. Lay them down, and when it's hard to part with them, ask for help. We all put back on the chains of our sin from time to time, but it's time to live as servants of God, where there are no chains, only grace.

ADDITIONAL READING: John 8:34–36; Romans 6:1–23

FROM HORIZON'S EDGE TO HORIZON'S EDGE

Who is a God like you,
forgiving iniquity and passing over rebellion
for the remnant of his inheritance?
He does not hold on to his anger forever
because he delights in faithful love.
He will again have compassion on us;
he will vanquish our iniquities.
You will cast all our sins
into the depths of the sea.
Micah 7:18–19

Early in adulthood, with a (tiny) margin of expendable income from my intern job (and the fact that I ate canned peas for dinner often), I set off with my roommate on a sell-out deal for a cruise. It was January, so the weather in the Caribbean was perfectly warm but never boiling, and the company was all living out their retirement on a big boat. I awoke early on our day at sea, and the deck was largely empty. I grabbed a cup of coffee and sat facing the glass barrier, sea as far as I could see. At this point, we were more than half a day away from land in any direction and it was as if the horizon never ended. East ran into west in an unending circle. Above the water stretched an unending sky.

Psalm 103:11–12 came to mind: "For as high as the heavens are above the earth, so great is his faithful love toward those who fear him. As far as the east is from the west, so far has he removed our transgressions from us." God's forgiveness of our sins is vaster than the horizons that meet or the expanse of the sky. The depths of the ocean are no match for the depths of God's forgiveness. As an early theologian said, "As a handful of sand thrown into the ocean, so are the sins of all flesh as compared with the mind of God."[12] Not only does God have the infinite power to forgive, He extends it, passing over rebellion and moving beyond anger to compassion again. Again and again, we rebel. And again and again, we see the beauty of the forgiveness of God that is free to all who would seek it in Christ. Who is like our God? Forgiving iniquity and passing over rebellion (v. 18)?

The only One who could forgive our sin (because He is the One we sin against) has chosen to do so. He could have responded in any other way, only extending wrath or reluctantly showing grace that comes with overwhelming guilt and a continuing grudge. He could have forgiven sin but kept a list close at hand to review each time we transgressed Him again. Instead, He sent His dearly beloved Son to take on our sin so that it could be hidden in Him forever.

Oh, how I wish I could be in the throne room as we confess our sin and Jesus steps in before the Father for us. We confess, and then Jesus affirms that He absorbed it and paid for it on the cross and the Father returns to our pleas asking, "What sin? It has already been thrown into the sea." What beauty in confessing, that He both knows and has already acquitted each one, throwing it as far as the east is from the west, the surface is from the deepest depths of the seas, and the heights of the heavens are from the earth.

You are a sinner, yes, but you are more so a saint, washed clean by the blood of Jesus and given new life, not the life of a prisoner to sin but a freedman to abundance in the presence of God. His forgiveness is great, but the lengths to which He went to establish it is greater. The benefits of Christ's work are great, but the work itself is greater. Contemplate the love of the Father, that He would provide costly forgiveness to you in exchange for your surrender to His good and right ways. He has saved you from yourself and your sin, a salvation that cost Him. How will you respond to Him today?

ADDITIONAL READING: Psalm 103:2–3; Luke 17:3–4; Acts 2:38; Ephesians 1:7; 1 John 1:9; Hebrews 9:22

13

A SAFE PLACE TO RUN

He said:
"The LORD is my rock, my fortress, and my deliverer,
my God, my rock where I seek refuge.
My shield, the horn of my salvation, my stronghold, my refuge,
and my Savior, you save me from violence."
2 Samuel 22:2–3

Golan, Ramoth, Bosor, Kedesh, Shechem, and Hebron: six cities every Israelite likely had memorized in case they needed them. Three on either side of the Jordan and scattered from north to south so that someone fleeing to them might get there quickly without the additional hardship of crossing the river. Six cities of refuge. Six communities ready to welcome the perpetrator of an accidental tragedy with open arms. Like the gates of the New Jerusalem, their gates were open day and night.[13]

God gave His people cities of refuge so that they wouldn't need to seek asylum in neighboring pagan nations for involuntary homicide. While murder was to be met with death according to the Law (Exod. 21:14), the person who caused death unintentionally had a safe place to go where an avenger of the deceased could not harm them. He would await trial there, and if the trial found that he did not kill intentionally, the city of refuge would become his permanent home, only able to return to his home of origin when the high priest died.

Each of these cities belonged to the tribe of Levi, those who had been chosen to serve the Lord in the temple as priests and attendants, and those whose portion was not land in Canaan like the other tribes, but their portion was God Himself (Deut. 18:1–8). The chosen priestly lineage of God would serve the refugee as unto the Lord, receiving them free of charge. In such a moment of personal tragedy—of both causing harm and then being forced to leave everything you know and love for a city of refuge—it would be a comfort to be with those who had been in the presence of God in the temple, as well as to know that these men chosen by God were righteous judges, hearing them out and caring for their needs.

These cities were a gift to God's people, and they also were a picture of what was to come through Jesus. Hebrews 6:17–19 seems to have these cities on its mind: "Because God wanted to show his unchangeable purpose even more clearly to the heirs of the promise, he guaranteed it with an oath, so that through two unchangeable things, in which it is impossible for God to lie, we who have fled for refuge might have strong encouragement to seize the hope set before us. We have this hope as an anchor for the soul, firm and secure. It enters the inner sanctuary behind the curtain." We are those who have fled to a city of refuge, even though our sin is certainly not always involuntary. Christ has acted as our Great High Priest, counseling us and declaring us innocent, not by our own account, but by His.

We can seize the hope set before us because Jesus has given His life for ours, His holy refuge in exchange for our sure death. He has saved us from the wrath we were due for our sin and has become our unshaken fortress in which we can hide and find life. God as our refuge does not simply mean He provides a strong structure, like a tornado shelter. He is not only a safe location in which we can rest, but He also provides for our needs and, through Christ, has found us innocent of every transgression.

If you are in Christ, no avenger or enemy can overtake your life because you are hidden in Him, and He is greater than any city of refuge. You have been led from your city of darkness to live forever in His city of light. You have nothing to fear because God is your rock, your fortress, and your deliverer.

ADDITIONAL READING: Nahum 1:7; Psalm 46:1–3; Psalm 91:9; Hebrews 13:6

14

INDIVISIBLE, BUT DISTINCT

Now it is God who strengthens us together with you in Christ,
and who has anointed us. He has also put his seal on us and
given us the Spirit in our hearts as a down payment.
2 Corinthians 1:21–22

Have you ever been tempted to think the Old Testament portrays the Father as full of wrath and judgment and the New Testament portrays the Son as full of grace and mercy? Or that the Spirit is the One who guides us while the Father is a sort of heavenly CEO? This is not the picture we find in Scripture that reveals the Oneness of God and the inseparable operations of His Persons. Father, Son, and Spirit—distinct in their relationship to one another—share in every attribute. This is not synonymous with how we might share a resource because our way of sharing is through division. Yet, the infinite cannot be divided. Each person is fully God and infinite in love, goodness, joy, justice, and so forth. There is nothing one Person of the Trinity does in which the other Persons don't also participate. Each Person is at work in our strengthening, our anointing, and our sealing. Our salvation is a work of the fullness of the Godhead.

The three Persons of God are impossible to separate, while also distinct. Father, distinct because He is eternally Father to the Son; Son, because He is eternally begotten of the Father; and Spirit, because He eternally proceeds from Father and Son. While our human minds may never fully comprehend it, we together can marvel in its beauty. The Persons of the Trinity are eternally with and within one another, and yet, they are still distinct, without blurring or blending.

When we see Jesus in the Scriptures, we don't try to look through His life into what God is like, as if He is a window. To look at Jesus is to see God in His fullness. He is not a lesser God than the Father or simply a picture of God. He is God, the only God there is, because He is One. To not affirm this moves us to tritheism, making God three different Gods who work together to achieve the purpose of the whole as if they are some cosmic basketball team. Rather, they share one will because they are together One, mutually indwelling one another. The term for this indwelling when we want to be very fancy is *perichoresis*, but it simply means that they are present within and with one another, affirming that there is no division of nature, will, or essence. This means you cannot have one of the Persons of the Trinity without having all three Persons. This is also why we can affirm without hesitation that to look at the Son is to look at God—to see clearly the will, essence, and nature of Father and Spirit in Him.

The mutual indwelling shared by the Trinity is the source of the glory of our participation in the divine life, that by being united with Christ we participate with Father, Son, and Spirit. This participation includes a vertical aspect of life with God and a horizontal aspect of life with His church. Both are transformative in your capacity to know and love God, miraculous as God redeems both your relationship with Him through your justification and your relationships with others through His sanctification.

Through the Son made flesh, God has invited you to participate in His divine life—a reality that is more real and concrete than what you can see and touch on earth. A quiet time is not just a task to complete, and church is not just an event on your calendar each week. These are opportunities to commune with Father, Son, and Spirit—to be in His presence, the place where heaven meets earth. To spend time with Him is to participate in His life and His mission. To know Him is to participate in eternity today. He is Father, Son, and Spirit, indivisible and perfectly simple. No imagination, ancient or modern, could develop such a glory. Only the one true God invites His people into communion with Himself by being three, by the Son taking on humanity so that we might be united to his humanity in our own. Glory to God—He did not send someone "like God," but God Himself. To look at Jesus is to see God. Fix your eyes on Him today.

ADDITIONAL READING: Matthew 9:5–6; Matthew 28:19–20; John 5:17, 19; John 14:8–10

AN EVER-PRESENT FATHER

See what great love the Father has given us that we should be called
God's children—and we are! The reason the world does not know us
is that it didn't know him. Dear friends, we are God's children now,
and what we will be has not yet been revealed. We know that when
he appears, we will be like him because we will see him as he is.

1 John 3:1–2

My childhood is marked by a present father. He placed lunches on bright pink plastic plates in the shape of faces, read *The Hobbit* out loud to me multiple times, patiently entertained my feeble attempts to play his guitar, and let me ramble on for hours without even a hint of disinterest. He loved to sit on the back porch, so I did too. I so wish those screened walls had recorded the conversations and laughter that happened inside them.

When my dad was diagnosed with cancer, I went to the cancer center with him every chance I got, and as an imaginative eight-year-old, I was sure I could figure out the cure, so I read about plants and remedies and he even entertained those ramblings. My dad navigated a tragic diagnosis with strength, and while he isn't with us anymore, the way he loved and lived helps me understand God as my Father better. In his absence, I also find that I'm consistently met with a heavenly Father who does not leave me alone in my grief. The senior daddy-daughter dance, graduations, my wedding day, when I take my kids to see my mom—these days have mingled grief and joy, alongside the peace of God, who is the Father to the fatherless.

I don't know what you picture in your mind when you consider your earthly father. I don't know if they were loving and attentive, absent, or abusive. Or maybe, like mine, he was simply gone too soon. Absent not by his choice but because his body gave out on him. I don't know the scars you carry from your childhood into how you think about God as Father, but I know that we all have them in varying degrees from even the most wonderful of parents. And I know this: God is the healer of scars and the perfect Father you did not have, because none are perfect.

The Old Testament reveals God as the Father who creates and sustains the world (specifically in Isaiah 63:16 and 64:8–9), but also as the Father of Israel. He wasn't simply their King. What King would bring manna from heaven so that His people would be fed? What King would call His people His treasured possession (Deut. 14:1–2)? He chose a covenant people for Himself, not just to lead them, but to also be their Father. It is not until the New Testament that we see Him as Father in all of His glory, sending His Son to rescue His sons and daughters who have turned away from Him. His Son reveals the Father more clearly than ever before in a language we can understand: His life.

There has never been a time when God was not Father. It is not like our ideas of earthly fathers and children, who share genetics but never time lines. There was never a time that the Son was begotten of the Father. They are outside of time and have always been—eternally—Father and Son within the triune God: Father, Son, and Spirit. He is innately relational within Himself, and this is foundational to all other truths about Him. The only way we know the Father is that we see the Son.

Yet as Jesus spoke of God as His Father, it appalled the listeners. How dare He make Himself equal with God and address Him in this too-close, too-familiar way when God is worthy of fear and trembling. It was even grounds for the Jews to plot to kill Jesus (John 5:18)! Yet the beauty of God as Father is glorious. This Fathering mirrored that of the day. They were integral to the provision of a family, and the future of his children's lives were dependent upon the passed down family business and inheritance. Also, fathers spoke blessings (or curses) over their children that charted their lifelong path (see Genesis 27 and Genesis 49). As children of God, He has spoken blessing over us in Christ, giving us good gifts and an immeasurable inheritance, providing for our forever future.

We have a perfect Father who is always near, always caring, always comforting, always listening, always kind, always gentle, always generous with His time and resources. The God who holds the stars in the sky and has planned and enacted a way of reconciliation, revealing His great mercy for His people, has chosen to enter a relationship with you, not as a distant King, although He is certainly worthy of worship and obedience. Instead, He is Father and this is your most real familial reality. He has prepared good for you, speaks good over you, and will usher you into eternal goodness when this age ends.

How would you describe your earthly father? Spend time reflecting on how God is unfathomably better in every way.

ADDITIONAL READING: Deuteronomy 14:1–2; Psalm 103:13; Isaiah 63:16; John 5:18; Galatians 4:6–7

THE POTTER OF THE CLAY

*Yet L*ORD*, you are our Father;*
we are the clay, and you are our potter;
we all are the work of your hands.
Isaiah 64:8

Adam was molded from the dust of the earth, shaped by the Father
through the eternally good hands that would also bear the scars of forgiveness after being stapled to the cross, the hands upon which the names of
the redeemed are written (Isa. 49:16). The Potter is remarkably near to His
clay—every divot, edge, and curve a result of His careful hand. These careful hands cut away in us what is not intended in His good plan and shape
us into the image of Christ, adding what we need to continue to be pliable,
like a potter at a wheel adding just the right amount of water as they work
the clay. This softness is necessary so that when pressure is applied, we might
not shatter under the weight of His hand.

The intention of this pressure is always for our good, strengthening
and reinforcing the walls of our hearts so that when the crushing weight
of living in a broken world falls upon us, we do not break. This process
is often unpleasant—the breaking down and building up of our lives, but

what gentleness the Potter has for us! We may be "afflicted in every way but not crushed; we are perplexed but not in despair; we are persecuted but not abandoned; we are struck down but not destroyed" (2 Cor. 4:8–9). This passage goes on to say: "We always carry the death of Jesus in our body, so that the life of Jesus may also be displayed in our body" (v. 10).

It is in the kiln of affliction that strength comes, glazed in the righteousness of Christ and put through the fire. He is teaching us His ways so that we may walk in them, shaped by the wise counsel of His Word and the Spirit's guidance as He indwells us. We are just clay jars, but we carry around the message that makes the dead alive and broken people whole. We are earthen vessels for everyday use, so that the good news of Jesus may be poured out and the light of Jesus may shine forth through the cracks or holes we once thought were the Potter's mistake.

No, the Potter does not make mistakes, and He does not work without intention. The intended use may be different, like the many clay pots used in the ancient Near East: some made for cooking, others for storing, and even others as oil lamps to light the night. He may even break you down or reshape you into something altogether new, but never without gentleness and intended good. He may shatter you so that He might repair you, like in the process of kintsugi, an ancient art of making broken pottery whole again through the laying of gold and lacquer into the cracks. Not only does this make the piece stronger, but it highlights the imperfections, also making it more beautiful. God is making and remaking you, and when your body finally returns to dust, the Christ you carry within will sustain you until He resurrects it again, remaking our fragile bodies into indestructible ones. Our Potter is intimately involved in all the workings of our life, and in His grace, He will be the One who restores us completely when He returns.

How have you seen God shaping you into the image of Christ? What might He use as tools in His hand to do the shaping? How are you being used as an everyday earthen vessel by Him today?

*God, may we trust Your hand to mold us into the image of Your Son
so that we might be vessels of light, made to carry the good news of
Jesus both in our hearts and for the world. Shape us, Lord. Crush
us, if You must. Do whatever it takes to keep us pliable. Teach us
Your ways and cultivate trust in our hearts so we may truly believe
our shaping is for our good. Teach us to be vessels that expand
Your kingdom and proclaim Your glory. In Jesus's name, amen.*

ADDITIONAL READING: Isaiah 29:16; Romans 8:29; 2 Corinthians 3:18

A FATHER'S REJOICING

*"The L*ORD *your God is among you,*
a warrior who saves.
He will rejoice over you with gladness.
He will be quiet in his love.
He will delight in you with singing."
Zephaniah 3:17

If ever there was an apt description of the father of my children right at their bedtime, it's this: "He is a warrior among you, fiercely protective as they recount the woes of their day, fiercely competitive in their pretend sword fights, pillow fights, and wrestling, and one who is quiet in his love, singing of his delight." Our home is often loud and chaotic one minute, then so still the next, as the tiniest child climbs into my husband's lap, snuggles up to him, and begins to drift off to sleep. Their father is both powerful and tender.

This is the image Zephaniah paints of the Lord who delights in His people: a warrior who doesn't fight with a pretend sword but as the ruler of all, the Lord of Armies, who holds all power and justice in His fist, and the Lord who is gentle, singing over His people with great love.

After harsh judgment for the rebellion of Judah, God promises to restore a remnant to Himself. Zephaniah reminded God's people that the day of judgment is coming, but that even judgment and discipline is good for the God who is infinitely good. A day is coming, Zephaniah promised, when God will replace His rebuke with rejoicing. He will deal with those who were oppressors, rescue the lame, and gather the exiles (v. 19). His promise is to bring His people home and restore their fortunes, giving them honor and praise (v. 20). This is the promise of a loving God who is both warrior and songwriter, protector and delighter. And while this particular promise was given to the faithful remnant of Zephaniah's time, if you are in Christ, you, too, are a part of the historic faithful remnant—those who enter through the narrow gate.

Through Christ, you have been made a child of God. You who were once a slave to sin and self have been set free through the work of Jesus, who has not only set you free, but allowed you to participate in God as you have been united to Him. John 1:12 says it this way: "But to all who did receive him, he gave them the right to be children of God, to those who believe in his name." Romans 8:17 goes on to say if we are children of God, then we are also heirs, or coheirs with Christ, sharing in His sufferings, which were for our sake, and in His glory, which is for our eternal good. We have received the same status as Jesus, the faithful, beloved servant and Son of God due to His obedience in our place—His obedience that covers our rebellion, if only we repent.

Though His people have historically suffered exile and oppression due to their rebellion, we suffer our own oppression and exile from God due to sin. Our Father who loves us has made a way to rescue us from ourselves and our sin. He fights for us, against the powers of evil and our own propensity to fall to its temptation, guiding us in the Spirit toward holiness and wholeness. A father who rejoices in his children views them not as a burden, but a blessing, enjoying them as they enjoy their father's presence. God sings over you, and He rejoices in your faithfulness.

God delights in you as a father who beams proudly as his toddler stumbles around, learning to walk. His expectations are not that you won't fall, but that you will continue to grow and learn, and soon, you'll run. You'll learn righteousness just like you learned to place one foot in front of the other.

There is no sin so terrible that you cannot be made right and no distance so great that you cannot come home to Him. With every step, cheers erupt. He has invited you to walk with Him and to take on His righteous and holy life, which leads to everlasting light and life. He is not a Father who is scowling, but is singing.

ADDITIONAL READING: Psalm 149:4; Isaiah 62:5; Romans 8:17

18

THE RUNNING FATHER: GOD'S COMPASSIONATE CARE

*"So he got up and went to his father. But while the son was
still a long way off, his father saw him and was filled with
compassion. He ran, threw his arms around his neck, and kissed
him. The son said to him, 'Father, I have sinned against heaven
and in your sight. I'm no longer worthy to be called your son.'
But the father told his servants, 'Quick! Bring out the best robe
and put it on him; put a ring on his finger and sandals on his feet.
Then bring the fattened calf and slaughter it, and let's celebrate
with a feast, because this son of mine was dead and is alive
again; he was lost and is found!' So they began to celebrate."*
Luke 15:20–24

In Luke 15:11–32, Jesus tells the story of a man with two sons. You may
know it as The Parable of the Prodigal Son, but I prefer what I've heard
it called more and more: The Running Father. This man had two sons, and
the younger requested that his father go ahead and give him his inheritance.
Now, this would be like yelling, "I wish you were dead!" right in his face.

This son was given that inheritance and he traveled to a distant country and squandered every cent. He became a hired hand in the pigpens, feeding the animals that he would have known to be unclean and wishing that he might share in their meal. He began to work out a path of repentance in his heart, determining to beg to be considered a servant in his father's house so that he might return. And yet, when he was far off, just a tiny speck on the horizon, his father recognized him. It would be customary for him to be turned away before he entered the village in which they dwelled. The leaders would meet him and make it clear that this son was not welcome to return, but not this father. Instead, he "was filled with compassion. He ran, threw his arms around his neck, and kissed him" (Luke 15:20). He instructed the servants to set up for a party to welcome him home, a feast of celebration. The son did not face condemnation, but compassion.

At this party, the older son who has continued to honor his father even while his younger brother was away feels as though his faithful obedience has been overlooked and underappreciated. He did not want to come into the party, yet, again, the father goes to him, pursues him. Leaving a party where you are the host would be shameful, but this father humbles himself so that his children may be brought near. Both the wayward son and the obedient son found the compassion of a pursuing father, one who put their needs of pursuit above his own of honor.

This is the character of God, our pursuing, compassionate Father. Whether we are more like the prodigal son or more like the self-righteous older son, God has met us with compassion; this compassion that welcomes us home, no matter how long we've been wandering, and meets us where we are, even when we are pouting or acting entitled. He is not an indignant, yelling father or a distracted, distant, uninvolved father. He is the pursuing, loving Father whose compassion leads Him to consistently seek to bring you back home to His loving fellowship and provision. He has laid our sins upon Christ on the cross, casting them as far as the east is from the west, and bidding us home to a right relationship with Him, not just begrudgingly opening His door to our knocking, but running to us. In Christ, we experience the fullness of His compassion. His mercies are new every morning; His faithfulness is unfailing. His care for His children is always full of compassion.

Have you traveled to a faraway land spiritually, squandering the good of God in your life? Are you lost despite not wandering far like the older brother, bitter and jealous? Oh, how great our rebellion, whether in grand show or a million tiny rebellions while we simultaneously seek to walk with Him. And despite our rebellion—despite ourselves—God comes running. Come home.

ADDITIONAL READING: Psalm 103:8; Joel 2:13; Luke 15:11–32; Romans 9:15–16

ADOPTED AS SONS

*"For you did not receive a spirit of slavery to fall back into fear.
Instead, you received the Spirit of adoption, by whom we cry
out, "Abba, Father!" The Spirit himself testifies together with
our spirit that we are God's children, and if children, also
heirs—heirs of God and coheirs with Christ—if indeed we
suffer with him so that we may also be glorified with him."*
Romans 8:15–17

In the ancient Near East, families were large and the plots of land they lived upon were relatively small. Sons shared the responsibility for tending the family's land and animals.[14] While they worked the land, it was nothing like the slavery that God's people knew in Egypt. In Egypt, fear was the currency of the day as slave masters saw little harm in bringing violence upon the people to move them to greater production. Thankfully, we are not slaves, we are sons—His children who have been given a blessing and an inheritance. He has transferred the rights and privileges of His Son to us through this action, making us righteous before Him and securing our identity as heirs of the kingdom of heaven, destined to receive the eternal blessings alongside Christ. And it's purposeful that the focus is sons because of their familial status in the ancient Near East. The sons were the glory of their father, continuing the family business, and receiving a blessing like Jacob received from Isaac (Gen. 27) or the twelve sons from Jacob (Gen. 49).

We aren't simply slaves treated like sons, but truly sons as Christ is Son. We have been brought near by the Spirit who has united our humanity with the humanity of Jesus, able to cry out "*Abba*, Father." This would be the first word little babies would say in Aramaic, crying out to their fathers in glee. Not sir, or master, or lord—while each would still be appropriate for the authority He holds, but *Abba*. This is a personal name, and we who were far away from Him could only be brought near enough to use it by the work of the Spirit to adopt us as children into the body of Christ.

Now, it's important that we are made sons rather than daughters because the rights and privileges held between the two differed greatly. The daughter was married off to another family, while the son was the one who stayed with his family, providing for them and receiving an inheritance upon his father's death. The Bible is not making a statement about males being better than females, but helping the readers at the time who were very familiar with these familial dynamics to see what was happening for the Christian relationally with God. He was near, lavishing upon His child "every spiritual blessing" (Eph. 1:3). We are coheirs with Christ, with the new heavens and new earth as our inheritance. God has gone to build a place for us in this eternal brightness that is to come, much like a father would build on to his house as needed to provide a space for his son when he married and their family grew. This is the family into which we have been adopted, not with additional disclaimers that explain how we entered, but with full acceptance by being united to Christ.

In the same way that my children all have the same responsibilities, rights, and privileges as our children, even though they didn't all enter our family the same way, we have been adopted into God's eternal family, joining in His business and dwelling in His house. You are a full member of the family of God, with its clearest outworking in the church, which is the outpost of the kingdom of heaven on earth. And in this family, we all look to the Father for provision and blessing, chief of which is Jesus, who has conquered the fear that once enslaved us, taking us not from slave to free but from slave to son.

My attempts to serve God often resemble my kids' lemonade stand. Even the cups and lemonade were purchased on my last grocery run. He is the Provider and the Preparer who has given you all access to Him. You have no less access, inheritance, or status than the Son of God. You have been brought near through His blood, adopted as sons.

Do you think God simply tolerates you? Do you think you are on some lower level than others who follow Him? You are His child—an equal heir. Ask Him to impress this upon your heart today.

ADDITIONAL READING: Psalm 68:5; John 14:18; Ephesians 1:3–6; Romans 8:14–17

NO POWER HE DOESN'T HOLD

"I know that you can do anything
and no plan of yours can be thwarted."
Job 42:2

Do you often carry the weight of the world on your shoulders? Do you live as though you are the one calling the shots; the one controlling what happens in your life, and if you work hard enough or smart enough that you can avoid suffering, secure protection and provision, and determine your every outcome? Or maybe it's easier to trust God's sovereign control for you, but not for your kids. You've got to be the all-present eyes and ears, ready to intercept them at any moment of danger.

I may be able to determine my steps for the day along with the substance that fills it, but I cannot add days. I cannot determine the steps of others that may derail my own. God has given us agency, but even that is simply a dim reflection of His better authority. He is in control, omnipotent—all-powerful. We participate with Him, making decisions and charting paths, but He holds the control. He allows us to join Him like a parent allows a child to choose what toy to play with next, and this is the abundant power that He holds across all people, all space, and all time, not just over our days or our lives, but everything both created and uncreated, visible and invisible, known to us and unknown to us.

By His infinite power, life springs forth at the sound of His voice. By His power, water changes to wine and the blind are healed. By His power, Jesus is brought from death to life in resurrection, and by His power we, too, will be raised. This is not a power that ebbs and flows like the tide but is constant—trustworthy. He is actively exercising His consistent power in the mundaneness of our days: the balance of the earth's temperature, the water cycle, and the careful control of the food chain. In His power, the sunrise is consistently painted, always rising somewhere in the world. He is the One who holds it in the sky, who commands its peaking over the horizon and returning behind it. His authority isn't authoritarian or militant, but because He is both powerful over all and knows all, every exercise of His sovereignty is good. There is no decision He makes that does not lead to life; no choice that does not bear good fruit.

If I was in charge, I'd make a huge mess of it all. My selfish ambitions and disordered intentions wouldn't just make my life more difficult, but would throw everything around me into chaos. Yet He also has the power over the chaos I may create. Not as an angry authority, but a loving, kind, rescuing, delivering authority—the highest power, the King of kings, full of grace and truth, life and light.

But what do we do when His ways look like death and darkness to us? How do we reconcile this authority with the trials of earth? Doesn't He have the power to do something? He does. And He has. And He will. God has promised that while we walk in this world so jaded by sin, we won't walk alone. He doesn't call evil good or good evil but rejoices in the truth. And we can rejoice in this truth: He is with us, and while sin has broken all things, it does not render God powerless or detract even an ounce from His sovereign control. Instead, in that power, He sent Jesus to conquer sin and death. All of the evil and ills of the world have an expiration date. Evil exists, but it has no power compared to the infinite, eternal power of God. In the chaos of life, the power of God is our constant, not because we won't face suffering but because we know the One who is authoritative over it. In what areas of your life are you seeking to control? Surrender to Him, as the One who has power over all, today.

> "We are not adrift in the chaos. We're
> held in the everlasting arms."[15]
> —Elisabeth Elliot, *Suffering Is Never for Nothing*

ADDITIONAL READING: Nehemiah 9:6; Isaiah 43:13; Jeremiah 32:27; Matthew 19:26

NO KNOWLEDGE HE
DOESN'T KNOW

Our Lord is great, vast in power;
his understanding is infinite.
Psalm 147:5

"Aren't two sparrows sold for a penny? Yet not one of them
falls to the ground without your Father's consent. But even
the hairs of your head have all been counted. So don't be
afraid; you are worth more than many sparrows."
Matthew 10:29–31

My favorite time of year begins as the ground begins to thaw. I linger at our picture window in the kitchen, looking for the birds that call our backyard home during the warmer months. They make a huge mess at our bird feeder sorting through the seed, throwing out what they don't want, but I don't care. They are beautiful—picky eaters—but beautiful: cardinals, goldfinches, wrens, and sparrows.

I watch for them, but God charts their flight patterns and their nesting location. He is fully aware of what they ate—or didn't—for breakfast out of our feeder. Not a single bird falls without His knowledge, even the sparrows—thought to be the smallest and least valuable bird in the time of Matthew's writing (two for just one copper coin or get five for two coins for our bargain shoppers [Luke 12:6]). And you are far more valuable than a sparrow. He knows your thoughts, actions, struggles, needs, and suffering. He knows every moment of history—past, present, and future—and how every person in every moment felt and responded. He even knows how our lives would unroll according to each of the options we are given, while also knowing exactly which one we will choose. He knows all and He knows you, both truly and fully. Nothing is hidden from Him, not even the deepest secrets of our souls. This knowledge would condemn us if not for Jesus's taking on of flesh—His perfect life, sacrificial death, glorious resurrection, and ascension. He knows our sins and secrets, yet He still cares for us.

This is a great comfort to the Christian and a great horror to those who are not covered by the righteousness of Christ. There is no junk drawer or cluttered closet in our hearts that God cannot access; no sin, no thought, no weak moment that is outside His gaze. He doesn't just know of our sin; He understands the motivations behind it. He doesn't just understand our needs; He knows precisely what is enough and what will leave us lacking. In His vast knowledge, He has chosen the confines of the world and the events of your life so that you might trust Him as the all-knowing, all-powerful, all-present God. He sees because He is all-knowing. He understands because He came in flesh, suffering precisely as we suffer.

His understanding is infinite. He doesn't just know all things, but He understands all things, able to think, plan, and act rightly because He never operates with partial information or faulty logic. His knowledge illuminates His power, as He does not guide blindly, but with full wisdom regarding both the largest movements of the world and the smallest, the curiosities of the guiding laws of space and the location of the fruit bushes He will lead my cardinals to late in the afternoon. And it's not just that He knows, but that He cares. Like God asking Adam and Eve where they were hiding when He already saw them clearly, He isn't looking for information; He's looking for those He loves. Are there sins hiding in the dark closets of your heart that need to be brought into the light today? God already knows them. He isn't looking for the information; He's looking for you. Are there areas of need? God already knows them, but He desires that you ask for what you need so that both in your need and provision, you learn to trust Him more. His wisdom knows no end.

ADDITIONAL READING: 1 Chronicles 28:9; Psalm 139:1–4; Hebrews 4:13

NO PLACE HE ISN'T

"Can a person hide in secret places where I cannot
see him?"—the LORD's declaration.
"Do I not fill the heavens and the earth?"—the LORD's declaration.
Jeremiah 23:24

It isn't always in the darkest days that God feels distant. In my darkest
days, when I lost my dad or when we lost a baby to miscarriage, God felt
near. Tragedy moved me to deep reliance on Him, and I had open eyes to
see His provision and presence in those moments. For me, God has often
felt most distant on the mind-numbing, dull days that seem to go on and
on. Whether you have felt distanced from God in obviously difficult days or
not so obviously difficult ones, you are not alone.

We know God is always everywhere, closer than the heart beating in our
chest, but His presence is not always manifested to us, or noticed. We don't
always feel His nearness because we were born into the overwhelming kindness of a God who is always everywhere. We can become desensitized to His
omnipresence, like a fish unaware of the water in which they swim. God's
omnipresence is so encompassing that it is not somehow confined by the
earth's atmosphere, but is both throughout the world and beyond, because

all is contained within Him. Tozer says it this way, "We think rightly about God and spiritual things only when we rule out the concept of space altogether. God, being infinite, does not dwell in space; He swallows up all space . . . God fills heaven and earth just as the ocean fills a bucket which has been submerged in it a mile down. The bucket is full of the ocean, but the ocean surrounds the bucket in all directions."[16] He does not only fill the heavens and earth, but He fills infinitely beyond them.

God is not bound within space; space is bound within Him. When we feel spiritually distant, we aren't talking about measurements of space like miles or inches.[17] Instead, we are calculating in terms of differentness—we are creature and He is Creator—there is a gulf between us, but this doesn't have to result in distance. God did not move away from us because of our sin; we moved away from Him. Really, we turned our back and ran in the opposite direction. And the only way back is Jesus.

The Creator took on creatureliness so that He may not be so different from us after all. The Son became like us so that we might become like Him, no longer separated from God because we are both found in Him and indwelled by the Spirit. We don't just experience God's presence outwardly, but also inwardly.

Wherever you go, God is there. And if you are in Christ, wherever you go, God also goes with you. You are like the bucket in the ocean, filled with His presence but also immersed in His presence. God is with you, and simultaneously with your brother or sister in Christ who is meeting in secret in the harshest of persecuted lands. He is truly with us, not philosophically, but in reality. This truth isn't a nicety we hope calms fear; it is the gospel truth we cling to as the truest truth—the most real reality.

God has promised that there is nowhere you can go that He is not. While the experience in the Holy of Holies and the temple courts was different in regard to His felt presence, He was no more with the high priest than He was the everyday worshipper. While the feeling of nearness may

ebb and flow, the actual presence of God does not. Spend some time asking God to pour out His manifest presence on your life today. Ask Him to
open your eyes to see Him, like a fish that suddenly understands they have
been swimming in an ocean full of water all along. Whether you are in your
darkest days or in mind-numbing mundane days, He is near. May we have
eyes to see.

ADDITIONAL READING: Psalm 139:7–10; Isaiah 57:15; Matthew 6:6

NO SHIFTING AND
NO SHADOWS

Every good and perfect gift is from above, coming down from the
Father of lights, who does not change like shifting shadows.
James 1:17

I can't name a single thing on earth that doesn't change, at least not a single thing that is alive. And those things that aren't alive will eventually decay too; it just takes longer. Because our view is so limited—our lives so vaporous—we often live as though this isn't true. We sink the structural supports of our lives into the shifting sands of earthly hopes, only to find no way to bear the weight when the winds blow. Nothing *here* is permanent, which feels so unsettling, but there—in the eternal City of God—all things are permanent: the place that is full of His fullness holds no change because He holds all in its God-assigned perfection for His God-accomplished glory. Permanence is what we long for—what I long for. I find myself often thinking: *If we could just reach this financial goal, I would never need to worry about money again* or *If we could just get on track with a healthy diet, I'd never have to worry about the potential of disease again.* Both of which are a fool's errand, an oasis in a vast desert of hopes and dreams that lures us in only to disappoint us. There is no "making it" with permanence because we are deeply dependent creatures.

The story of God's people is a story of consistent inconsistency and dependency. As quickly as they chose to turn back from their idols to the God who had always been for and with them, they'd be back to their old ways, making golden cows in the wilderness, allowing the ark to be taken by the Philistines, doing whatever is right in their own eyes. God wasn't robotic in His emotions and responses to these moments, as if constancy equates to stagnation or coldness. Instead, He is never unreasonably angry, unpredictably irritable, or unengaged and avoidant of His people. He is unchanging; His path to wholeness through Jesus is unchanging; and His welcoming home of sinners is unchanging. In a world that ever changes, He is permanent, and He is building a kingdom of permanence that will have no end.

The hymn writer, Jennie Wilson, wrote a beautiful, simple song called "Hold to God's Unchanging Hand," a call for us all today. It says:

> Time is filled with swift transition.
> Naught of earth unmoved can stand.
> Build you hopes on things eternal.
> Hold to God's unchanging hand.
>
> Hold to His hand, God's unchanging hand.
> Hold to His hand, God's unchanging hand.
> Build your hopes on things eternal.
> Hold to God's unchanging hand.
>
> Trust in Him who will not leave you.
> Whatsoever years may bring.
> If by earthly friends forsaken,
> Still more closely to Him cling.

Hold to His hand, God's unchanging hand.
Hold to His hand, God's unchanging hand.
Build your hopes on things eternal.
Hold to God's unchanging hand.[18]

The sands may shift under your feet, but He will not remove His hand. He will not let go of you. He will not change. He does not lie, shift, or manipulate. He is God. He is good. And He is unchanging.

Are you holding on to things that degrade in decay instead of the One who is unchanging? Are you afraid to hold on to Him because He might change His mind about you? He won't. He is constant. He will always welcome you home. Your hope is sure today because your God doesn't change.

What are the implications for your life that the God you serve is unchanging? Why does this matter *today* for you?

ADDITIONAL READING: Psalm 102:27; Malachi 3:6; Hebrews 13:8

24

HOLY, HOLY, HOLY

And one called out to another:
Holy, holy, holy is the LORD of Armies;
his glory fills the whole earth.
Isaiah 6:3

I saiah 6 recounts an incredible vision of the glory and holiness of God. Isaiah saw the Lord on His throne, and His temple was filled with His robe. Winged creatures stood above Him, shouting His holiness (6:3), and the foundation was shaken at their call. When a phrase or word is repeated in Scripture, pay attention because the author is highlighting the importance of that truth. Here, "holy" is repeated three times, emphasizing God's perfect holiness. The radiance of this holiness fills the whole earth as His glory, which is the beauty of who He is in that same perfect holiness.

Isaiah's immediate response to the holiness of God—the perfect purity and ultimate separateness of God—is to cry out about his uncleanness. He says, "Woe is me for I am ruined because I am a man of unclean lips and live among a people of unclean lips, and because my eyes have seen the King, the LORD of Armies" (v. 5). Isaiah is overwhelmed by God's holiness, which has illuminated his lack of it, his impurity. He is unclean in the presence of the perfectly clean.

So if God is so perfectly holy, how can He call us to be the same? He says, "Be holy, because I am holy" (Lev. 11:44–45; 1 Pet. 1:15–16). How can our hearts seek not our own desires, but be aligned with God's? Can we be holy on our own account, hating what is evil and loving what is good? His Law revealed what is good, while also condemning us in our inability to keep it. The holy presence of God in the Holy of Holies could only be entered once a year on the Day of Atonement, but not without the right preparations and "never without blood" (Heb. 9:7). Sin was so terrible—so marring of the purity of God—that only death in the place of the sinner could make one pure again. Only the clean could come into the temple to worship, and yet . . . Jesus turns this world of constant focus on clean and unclean upside down.

When those with skin diseases were being sent outside the camp because of their uncleanness—completely avoided by those who were considered clean—Jesus sought them out and touched them (Luke 5:12–16). When a woman who had been bleeding for twelve years came to Jesus, she touched the hem of His clothes and immediately was healed. Yet He was not affected like another might be when the unclean touched Him. His infinite holiness does not allow that He be overcome by the uncleanness. Instead, He touches the unclean and makes them clean—the opposite of the human experience, the reverse of the curse. Jesus went on to defeat the markers of uncleanness—disease and death—and one day, He will destroy them for good. When we could not "be holy, because I am holy," Jesus was holy in our place, making us clean with His blood. As those who trust Him, our truest reality is that we lived His perfectly obedient life alongside Him, crucified and resurrected, now "seated with him in the heavens" (Eph. 2:6). We are holy because Jesus is holy. There is no necessary striving, only growing up into what we already are in Him, growing to hate evil and love what is good.

And in His great goodness, we have become His temple, the Holy of Holies where He dwells. You are holy, so be holy, not on your own because you will surely fail, but by looking to the Holy One, by asking Him to purify you.

How do you need God to purify your heart and your mind today?

ADDITIONAL READING: Exodus 15:11; Isaiah 57:15; Revelation 15:4

BEAUTY OF THE BEHOLDEN

*I have asked one thing from the LORD; it is what I desire: to
dwell in the house of the LORD all the days of my life, gazing
on the beauty of the LORD and seeking him in his temple.*
Psalm 27:4

Every Sunday for at least a decade of my life, we ended each service with one of three hymns. My favorite goes like this: "Turn your eyes upon Jesus. Look full in His wonderful face. And the things of earth will grow strangely dim in the light of His glory and grace."[19]

This beautiful hymn, also known as "The Heavenly Vision," was written by Helen H. Lemmel. She was born in 1863 in Europe, later moving to the United States after meeting her husband at age forty-three. She became a music teacher at Moody Bible Institute, and shortly after, she developed an illness that took her sight. Her husband struggled with her malady, abandoning her in her darkest moments. Yet, despite the crushing tragedies she walked through, her faith held strong, looking to the day that she would once again see, and the first face her eyes would gaze upon would be her Savior. Eyes that are unable to take in the light of the sun would one day take in the eternal light of the Savior that illuminates His face. Her blindness is but a vapor—just for a moment—ending in the greatest reward: the beauty of Christ, her Savior.[20] And today, we may gaze upon His beauty, if only a glimpse, seeing the earth for what it truly is: dim and unsatisfying in light of His beauty, because to see Him is to know Him fully.

There is nothing that is less than beautiful about God, nothing that is not good. He is both the Creator of all beauty and Beauty itself, as anything we deem beautiful somehow reflects His glorious handiwork, and our eyes see its beauty due to His light. Do you find the beauty of God more enrapturing than the dim reflections we see in the world? The beauty of earth fades in our aging eyes, but God is unchanging. His glory is so radiant, that He placed Moses in the cleft of a rock, only allowing him to see His back because His back was all Moses could handle of God's glory (Exod. 33:18–23). It is so wonderful that those who met with Him on the mountain shone (Exod. 34:29). As His people wandered in the wilderness, worshipping in the tabernacle and later the temple, the priests could only enter God's beautiful, glorious presence once a year in the Holy of Holies in a temple that proclaims His beauty with the handiwork of its construction, creative gifts specifically given by God for this purpose.

And then, God takes on flesh. An ordinary-looking man holds the beauty of God in His hands (Isa. 53:2b). This Savior who is both God and man, would willingly go to the cross for us, an act more beautiful than all the world's riches. It's through Him the riches were created, and it's through Him that the most beautiful story may be told: God provided a way for us to be right with Him through the glorious blood of His Son, and there is a day when He will return with hair like wool, eyes like flames, and feet like bronze (Rev. 1:13–15). He will usher us into a garden-city, to which even the most beautifully cultivated garden cannot begin to compare. The most beautiful gems and gleaming gold fail to describe. Cathedrals of old were crafted across lifetimes to proclaim the current and coming beauty of God, the beauty of His presence with His people when they meet to worship

Him. And one day, it will be fully realized and those cathedrals will look like quickly drawn sketches, just a shadow of the Artist's fullness.

His beauty is seen, even if our sight fails. And His beauty is what will reverberate across the time and space of eternity. Beauty is not in the eye of the beholder, but in the One whom we behold. He is the Light through whom all sight and perception exists—and oh how bright that Light is for those who choose Him over the temporary beauties of the world. Helen wrote it well: "O soul, are you weary and troubled? No light in the darkness you see? There's light for a look at the Savior, And life more abundant and free!"[21] Fix your eyes on the Beautiful One, and the troubles and even the triumphs of this life will grow strangely dim. We know beauty because we know Him.

ADDITIONAL READING: Revelation 21:1–5, 9–26; Revelation 22:1–5

LOVE WITH NO CONDITIONS

And we have come to know and to believe the love that
God has for us. God is love, and the one who remains
in love remains in God, and God remains in him.
1 John 4:16

I'd be shocked if 1 Corinthians 13:4–8a isn't the most read passage in Christian weddings, and it is a worthy goal to seek within marriage, but it is not specifically about the love between two broken people. Instead, the Greek word translated as love in this passage is *agape*, the unconditional, unending love of God. This passage says, "Love is patient, love is kind. Love does not envy, is not boastful, is not arrogant, is not rude, is not self-seeking, is not irritable, and does not keep a record of wrongs. Love finds no joy in unrighteousness but rejoices in the truth. It bears all things, believes all things, hopes all things, endures all things. Love never ends."

This is not the love that ebbs and flows with the flights of stomach butterflies or the slow wane of distanced friends, but love without condition or end. We struggle to describe it because true love is not a human faculty, but a divine gift. To know God is not to simply experience His actions of love, but to know Love. God is love. Because He is not made up of a host of characteristic "parts," but is perfectly unified as One, it's not that love trumps His other attributes, but that they are perfectly one also—inseparable. His love and justice cannot be pitted against one another because they are not separate parts of God, but one. He is loving because He is just, and He is just because He is loving. He cannot be unloving—not because that is what God is like, but because that is who God *is*. He creates in love; He rejoices in love; He provides in love; He disciplines in love.

How might we live if we truly came to know and believe the love of God? The love that is beyond comprehension, that would move Him to send His Son to redeem His rebellious ones? Jesus was always God's plan for the redemption of His people because His great love—who He is—could not be sovereign over a broken world without a path for reunification. He has loved us, the unlovable, since before there was time. In our deepest moment of need, God has made a way for us. There is no earthly love that compares to the depth of His perfect, infinite love. This is the love that holds us to Him, even when we let go. It is not our love—the imperfect, often conditional, here-today-gone-tomorrow love that is so easily influenced by the happenings of the day. It is His. There is no sin so great it turns away His love from you.

There is no season of wandering so long and no situation so broken that His love cannot redeem. When you were incapable of choosing Him, He chose you. His love holds no condition. You don't have to be good enough for Him. He is both infinitely loving and perfectly sinless, so His love is never dimmed by a less than right and good response to us as His children. There is nothing that He won't walk through with you. He will never wash His hands of you or give up on you. You were at the bottom of the deep pit of your sin; He found you and offered you rescue: "No one has greater love than this: to lay down his life for his friends" (John 15:13). Jesus is God's love to us—His redemption, our glory.

In a world that rewards cynicism and lashing out at those who might disagree with you, God drew near to those who were living in active rebellion to Him. He sent His Son to eat with sinners and to heal the sick. "We love because he first loved us" (1 John 4:19), and His perfect love casts out fear. You are deeply loved by the Lord of heaven and earth. There is nothing more we need. We know the fullness of His love in Christ. His love lights the darkest caverns of the soul. You are loved.

ADDITIONAL READING: Deuteronomy 7:9; 1 John 4:7–12

RIGHTING EVERY WRONG

The Rock—his work is perfect;
all his ways are just.
A faithful God, without bias,
he is righteous and true.
Deuteronomy 32:4

God is the rock of justice—the unmoved, the unchanged, the weighty. Yet his justice flows from His character like the water that flowed from the rock to quench the thirst of the Israelites in the wilderness. The injustices of today leave us rightfully thirsty for God to intervene, releasing the floodwaters of His great justice, crashing into oppression and mistreatment so that all may be made right in its rushing. While injustice abounds and it seems as though our sin has built dams to avoid His just movement, it is grace that we, too, are not swallowed in its undertow.

God's justice, and His delay in bringing what we believe to be justice in this world rife with strife, is wholly an act of love. While we desperately thirst for His justice to wash over us, begging God to do something—anything—His Word quietly whispers, "He has. And He will." All injustice finds its answer in Christ, the One on whom God's wrath was poured so that we might faithfully affirm that vengeance is the Lord's, a vengeance that those who are united to Christ will not face. Every wrong has been righted through the blood of Jesus, and now we wait for that work of justice to be completed. His righteous hand has been set against the schemes of the Enemy, and not one of them will prevail.

His justice is not opposed to His love, as though He could be divided within Himself. Instead, His justice flows from His love, making right the wrongs done to the people and world God loves. It is because of His love that He will bring judgment to those who are lords of injustice in our world today, and He will redeem every brokenness brought about by the sins of another. We cannot enact His justice perfectly because our sin taints us. We cannot be perfectly unbiased or even claim to know in whole what steps toward justice are needed, but we can pray His kingdom come. His will be done. His justice for us and for those we love. His justice for our churches, our cities, and our world.

In the Old Testament, lost battles and lost lives, exile and enslavement came as a result of the outpouring of God's wrath, a just movement of God in response to His people who transgressed His law and loved their idols far more than they loved God. God gave chance after chance for them to return to Him, and in His love, He undammed His justice for just a moment. He created difficulties for them so they might see and know Him, so they might love Him because all of His ways are light and life. These exercises of His justice are cautionary tales for our righteous living as He promises to do likewise for those who practice evil.

We do not see the arc of history in a single glance, but God does. And its culmination is found in the justice enacted on the cross. The just punishment for sin is death, and it is what every one of us deserves, but God, in love, poured out His just wrath on His Son, bringing us life. Removing us from those destined for His just wrath and hiding us in the glorious Savior who has made all things right through the breaking of His body and the spilling of His blood. This secures us in His grace, without need for vengeance for our sin to fall upon us, because it has been absorbed by Jesus.

While there is no lack of injustice in any corner of the world, God has and will right it through Christ. He turns over tables and chases out the ones who take advantage of His people (Matt. 21:12–13), and He will execute His righteous anger—His righteous judgment—when He returns. And while we wait, our charge is to echo His justice so that it might reverberate throughout every land and people. As people of light, our good goal is to advocate for the oppressed and stir up justice, making each moment on earth a little more like heaven as we await His return.

Have you been wronged? Thank God that He will right it all. Have you done wrong? Thank God that your sin has been absorbed by Christ on the cross. His justice has been executed in Christ for those who love Him.

ADDITIONAL READING: Job 37:23; Psalm 89:14; Amos 5:24; Zephaniah 3:5; Romans 12:19

BOTH TRANSCENDENT AND NEAR

The LORD is exalted above all the nations,
his glory above the heavens.
Who is like the LORD our God—
the one enthroned on high,
who stoops down to look
on the heavens and the earth?
He raises the poor from the dust
and lifts the needy from the trash heap
in order to seat them with nobles—
with the nobles of his people.
Psalm 113:4–8

L ike the Israelites demanding an earthly king to match the nations around them, we, too, forget the beauty and goodness of being led by Someone who is wholly unlike His creation, who is transcendent. The One who is above all the nations and enthroned on high is perfectly perfect, infinite in all His attributes, unlimited in all His ways. He is better than our finite minds can imagine. Yet, like Eve in the garden, we wonder: *Is it true? Or should I know all so that I might monitor His ways? So that I might be the judge of His intentions?* How highly we think of ourselves, forgetting that God who is transcendent over all, who is set apart and different from His creation, fashioned us with His hands. God is greater, superior to all. His thoughts are not our thoughts, and his ways are not our ways (Isa. 55:8).

He is higher, but not in reference to His location, as if He might be confined by space. He is not geographically above us, whether in terms of north and south or in terms of being located in space or beyond it. These are categories we use to better understand in our human faculties, but there is no category that can contain God. He is beyond our human faculties and unlike anything on earth.

This same God who is exalted above the heavens and wonderfully different from us is also near, stooping down to look on heaven and earth. Not that He must crouch to see as if He's a giant with His head in the clouds, but that His splendor brings Him to make Himself low so that He might commune with His creation. The Father is near to the dust from which He has raised us—poor and needy. He is not repelled or disgusted by imperfect and impure people. Instead, He draws ever nearer through His Son.

It is in this bending down to humanity that Jesus enters. God Himself takes on flesh, humbling Himself and coming close to the dirt from which He created man, looking us in the eyes with unending love. He stooped down to be with us in flesh, taking on what ails us so that He might truly heal it; so that He might be the image of what humanity was meant to be without sin. Gregory of Nazianzus said it this way: "For that which He has not assumed He has not healed."[22] He took on flesh so that our flesh might be made whole. He became man so that man might know and love Him. He has raised us to the place of nobility because that is His place, and His work of redemption is a work of swapping places with us—giving us His place of nobility and taking on the trash heap of sin we dwelled in for so long.

He has brought light and life, peace and hope into a world of desperation. He has taken us—orphans and foreigners—from seeking nourishment among the trash heap of striving and suffering to the table of nobles with Him as our Bread of Life. He is transcendent, but He is also immanent, crossing the divide of creature from Creator and revealing that He both knows us and is able to be known by us. God has come near. He isn't simply aware of our burdens; He has taken them on Himself. He hasn't come to remove our humanity, but to make us truly human and whole, with His life as the model. He has both assumed flesh and healed it.

He has not rescued us out of our situation; He has come to live it with us, both in Christ and in the Spirit who unifies us with Christ. The sufferings of today may attempt to place us back into the dust or the trash heap, but the hope and peace of Christ compels us to live in our truest reality: that spiritually, we are seated with Him as nobility, cared for by Him in every way. He has come near even in His great transcendence, and His presence is good.

God, Your presence is our peace. Your presence
is our promise. Make us whole.

ADDITIONAL READING: Job 38–42; Psalm 145:18; Isaiah 55:8–9; Haggai 2:5; Romans 11:33–36

NEW EVERY MORNING

Because of the LORD's faithful love
we do not perish,
for his mercies never end.
They are new every morning;
great is your faithfulness!
Lamentations 3:22–23

The words of this lament were penned by Jeremiah, who is known as the weeping prophet. First, he brought the news of horrifying judgment, that God would bring exile by way of the Babylonians if they chose to continue in their ways. These people Jeremiah loved had turned their back on God and refused to heed his warnings. King Jehoiakim burned the scroll that contained his prophecy (Jer. 36), and the men of Anathoth threatened to kill Jeremiah if he didn't stop bringing the message of the Lord (Jer. 11:18–23). Even his family sought to harm him (Jer. 12:6). He was also accused of treason and imprisoned in a pit of mire (Jer. 38) and put into stocks for a day to be mocked and beaten (Jer. 20:1–2). He didn't just warn the people of exile, he lived it with them in real time. This was a difficult, full-of-sadness-and-tears calling of God. Every day, he obeyed, and every day it seemed, there was a new suffering that came as a result of that obedience.

Jerusalem has been made an empty, desolate city, ransacked by the Babylonians. In Jeremiah's great sadness, He turns his eyes to the faithfulness of the Lord, praising Him for the mercy He has extended, despite their judgment. His mercies are a happy companion in the days of ease, but a life-saving bandage and balm in great trial. There's a desperation for this daily mercy, a reliance on it that only comes through hardship, knowing it is only by God's love that we do not perish because that is what our sin deserves, and only by His mercies each morning that we are sustained. The anguish of sin is lightened in the kindness of His mercy.

We know mercy only because God has revealed it to us through Christ. He is the ultimate substitution for us so that we might experience God's mercy, paying our debt with His blood. While judgment will still come for those who do not know Him, we who do will always and forever experience God's eternal mercies. He has done for us what we do not deserve in our time of desperation, when even judgment would be merciful because of the great abomination of our sin. Even judgment that we experience on this side of the coming final day of judgment holds the hope of restoration. On that day, God's sovereignty and justice will determine the exercising of His mercy.[23] As God told Moses, and Paul repeated, "I will show mercy to whom I will show mercy, and I will have compassion on whom I will have compassion. So then, it does not depend on human will or effort but on God who shows mercy" (Rom. 9:15–16). Even His judgment is merciful, because even the worst punishment for sin is not equal to the abomination of sin.

Of course, He has ultimately revealed mercy to us in the life of Jesus, the One who took on the punishment we deserved so that we might experience eternal mercies. Our debt has been paid. Through Jesus, mercy may be given rightly and justly to those who love Him because He has taken on the penalty of our sin. Only mercy remains. He has done for us what we do not deserve, sustaining our breath and causing us to open our eyes each morn-ing, even if the breaths are labored in fear or the eyes are difficult to open in exhaustion. What are the desperate places in your life that need God's new mercies? Where can you cry, despite the hardship, "Great is your faith-fulness! Your mercies never end!" His mercies are truly unending in their supply, unlimited in God's generosity to give it freely. New every morning.

ADDITIONAL READING: Deuteronomy 7:9; Psalm 25:10; Jonah 3:10; Luke 1:78; Ephesians 2:4–5

BEGOTTEN, NOT MADE

"For God so loved the world, that he gave his only
begotten Son, that whosoever believeth in him
should not perish, but have everlasting life."
John 3:16 KJV

This is how I memorized John 3:16 as a child, and I imagine many of you did as well. Other translations update "begotten" to His "only Son," but the word *begotten* is an important one. Begotten describes Jesus's relationship to the Father, the relationship that has been true of them since eternity past and will be true into eternity future. We know Father and Son by their relationships within the Trinity.

In John 8:48–59, Jesus claimed to be God's Son, seeking the Father's glory and able to give eternal life to those who keep His word. These claims were so shocking the teachers of the Law thought He surely had a demon. He claimed that anyone who keeps His word will never see death (v. 49), a claim only God could make. He claimed God as His Father (v. 54), and that Abraham "rejoiced" to see his day (v. 56). Then, Jesus really shocked them. He claimed: "before Abraham was, I am" (v. 58). Both eternal, as one seeing Abraham who lived some two thousand years earlier, and even more shocking, the I AM, the way God introduced Himself to Moses from the burning bush (Exod. 3:14). These final claims caused the listeners to pick up stones, ready to throw them at Jesus, but by the time they picked them up, Jesus was gone.

If these claims are true, how are they reconciled with what God's people had believed since God called Abraham (Gen. 12) and spoke to Moses from the burning bush (Exod. 3)? The early church grappled with these questions, working to better understand the person and nature of Jesus. The KJV's use of "begotten" in John 3:16 is used throughout the Old Testament in the many family trees and censuses recorded. Jesus is God's Son, but not like your son or the sons you know. While Jesus was carried in His mother's womb and born as a son to a young Mary, the truth of His identity reached infinitely in the past before He was swaddled tightly and placed in a feeding trough. Before the Son took on flesh, He was present with the Father, and before the Son took on flesh, He was eternally coexisting with the Father—sharing in His essence and will. The Father is the Father because He is eternally the Father of the Son, and likewise, the Son is the Son because of His eternal relationship to the Father.

So what is the origin of the Son? There has never been a time that the Father was without the Son—never a time that He was created or formed into the Son. In the fourth century, the early church struggled to put words to truth with this doctrine because there is not one clear biblical text that spells it out precisely for us. They wrestled with the language of these truths, providing statements at church councils to help us in our understanding. The Nicene Creed is among those statements, and it is an affirmation of the Son as eternally generated or coming forth from the Father's essence. The Father communicates the essence of God to the Son in this eternal, internal act. He is equal in every way to the Father, and there is no hierarchy within the Trinity. Without eternal generation, we erase the beauty of the simplicity and diversity of God within the Godhead, that He is both One and distinctly Three.

While we might use the term *begotten* to describe human sonship, the only "begotten" Son of the Father had no beginning and will have no end. Jesus entered time and space into the tight confines of His mother's womb, but this is not His beginning. Instead, He was generated by the Father before time, in eternity past. It is not His taking on flesh that makes Him the Son, but His eternal generation. He is outside of time, unbound by its linear requirements. Eternal generation isn't something that happens *to* the Son, but something the Son simply is.

This was hotly debated by Athanasius (who argued that the Son is of the same substance as the Father) and Arius (who argued that the Son is of a like substance as the Father). Arius knew his Bible and sought to honor Christ, but he was wrong. Unfortunately, many Christians fall into believing with him that Jesus is wonderful, but still a little different—a little lower—than the Father. That is not the picture we see in Scripture. Instead, it's as the early church fathers declared it in 325 at the Council of Nicaea. Return to page 25 and read it again.

He is God of God, Light of Light—the eternally generated begotten Son who is one with the Father and Spirit, and He has secured our salvation. He is good.

ADDITIONAL READING: Matthew 22:41–46; John 8:48–59

SON OF GOD

Paul, a servant of Christ Jesus, called as an apostle and set apart
for the gospel of God—which he promised beforehand through
his prophets in the Holy Scriptures—concerning his Son, Jesus
Christ our Lord, who was a descendant of David according
to the flesh and was appointed to be the powerful Son of God
according to the Spirit of holiness by the resurrection of the dead.

Romans 1:1–4

Descended according to the flesh from Adam, Israel, and David, Jesus is appointed according to the Spirit, because that which has eternally existed cannot suddenly be a descendant of another. In His humanity, He is the descendent of Adam, inheriting His humanity from Mary, while in His deity, He is the appointed of the Spirit, conceived by Him in the womb of Mary, but not originated there. He had no earthly father, but truly is the Son of God, with God as His Father. It is this relationship that most clearly differentiates the Persons of the Trinity: Father, Son, and Spirit—the Father begets the Son, and the Father and Son spirate or "breathes out" the Spirit.

The Son has always been begotten by the Father—not in time, but outside it, eternally generated before the beginning. And Jesus has always been the Son. There wasn't a time when Jesus "took on" the divine. He didn't need to reach a certain age or level of holiness before God was willing to join His deity to Jesus's humanity. Jesus was not a great man who God saw was holy like Noah or Abraham, so He decided it was an appropriate time to launch His plan for redemption alongside this trustworthy, righteous human. No, Jesus was not a man adopted by God, but is God Himself—God the Son who is the Son of God.

Luke 4:40–41 details Jesus healing the sick and casting out demons, and as He would lay His hands upon the suffering person, the demons would come out of them, shouting, "You are the Son of God!" Even the demons knew this title of Jesus, but more than the title, they knew it to be true. This is the Son of God who has authority over all, so if He told the demons to depart, they must leave. Even beings that would never willingly worship Him proclaim the truth of His deity as He casts them out. The Father even spoke this truth over Jesus at His baptism in Matthew 3, as it says in verses 16–17: "When Jesus was baptized, he went up immediately from the water. The heavens suddenly opened for him, and he saw the Spirit of God descending like a dove and coming down on him. And a voice from heaven said, "This is my beloved Son, with whom I am well-pleased." The Son of God had come to dwell with—and to serve—His people, beginning His ministry after this anointing of the Spirit and this declaration of His Sonship.

Paul also discussed Jesus as the Son of Man in a beautiful passage, Galatians 4:4–7. It says, "When the time came to completion, God sent his Son, born of a woman, born under the law, to redeem those under the law, so that we might receive adoption as sons. And because you are sons, God sent the Spirit of his Son into our hearts, crying, "*Abba*, Father!" So you are no longer a slave but a son, and if a son, then God has made you an heir." Because Jesus is God's Son, you also get to share in His Sonship, being made an heir through union with Jesus, united in your humanity to His humanity, able to commune with the Father because of His status as Son that He shares with you. We are made right with God because Jesus is the Son of God. If He was only man, we would still be lost in our sin, because someone who was only man could not overpower the curse upon humanity as those bent toward sin. Only God could stand against temptation as Jesus did. Only God could calm storms and heal the sick. And only God could forgive sin.

The title of Son of God is often contrasted with the title Son of Man, but it is not the contrasts that are most important, but their concurrence. Both must be true for our salvation to be sure; Jesus must be both God and Man—or Son of God and Son of Man. He is not a Son like you may be a son or your son may be your son. But He is fully participating with the Father and Spirit as One. He is the Son of God, worthy of our worship and the King of a kingdom that will never end. May we live today in light of our King's never-ending reign, full of joy because the Son has also made us heirs.

ADDITIONAL READING: John 1:1–18; Romans 5:14; 1 Corinthians 15:45; Hebrews 2:10

SON OF MAN

I continued watching in the night visions,
and suddenly one like a son of man was
coming with the clouds of heaven.
He approached the Ancient of Days
and was escorted before him.
He was given dominion
and glory and a kingdom,
so that those of every people, nation,
and language should serve him.
His dominion is an everlasting dominion
that will not pass away,
and his kingdom is one
that will not be destroyed.
Daniel 7:13–14

Daniel is one of the only Old Testament books that includes apocalyptic elements, similar to the book of Revelation. It's an interesting mix of narrative about being exiled in Babylon and unusual happenings and references that point forward to what will happen at the Day of the Lord. There is a hand writing on a wall in the palace (Dan. 5:5–6) and visions of the end, like the one above in Daniel 7. Daniel ends up in a lion's den and his friends end up in a furnace. It's a wilder ride than the latest box office hit.

In Daniel's vision in chapter 7, he sees "one like a son of man [who] was coming with the clouds of heaven" (v. 13). He then goes on to tell us about this Son of Man: he would be given dominion (just as Philippians 2 says of Jesus), as well as glory and an everlasting kingdom so that every people would serve Him. You'll likely find this passage strangely familiar, even if you haven't spent much time in Daniel, because the New Testament writers often use this language to help the reader understand that this Son of Man Daniel writes about is indeed Jesus.

In the four Gospels, this title is used seventy-eight times, almost always by Jesus referring to Himself. This is who He knew Himself to be: the Second Adam (the son of the first man) and the fulfilment of the prophecies. This title highlights His humanity, but also positions Him as the representative for all humanity. He is the Son of Man, which in Hebrew would read *ben adam* (*adam* means human or humankind, so this title could be translated as Son of Man or Son of Adam).[24] He has come as the Second Adam, the One who was mature and chose obedience in the garden of Gethsemane rather than the one who was immature and chose rebellion in the garden of Eden. He is "the man," the new representative of true humanity, the perfection of Adam.

This Son of Man, as portrayed in Daniel 7, cannot only be man if He is to be the King of an everlasting kingdom because the curse of death would see to it that all kingdoms end. Instead, it is further promised that the Son of God would become the Son of Man, taking on flesh and dwelling among us. While He would be man, He would not give up His deity. He confirmed both in Matthew 26:63b–64: "The high priest said to him, 'I charge you under oath by the living God: Tell us if you are the Messiah, the Son of God.' 'You have said it,' Jesus told him. 'But I tell you, in the future you will see the Son of Man seated at the right hand of Power and coming on the clouds of heaven.'" This is a direct tie to Daniel 7:13–14, and the high priest and all others who were listening as he challenged Jesus would recognize this passage.

Even Pilate announces Jesus as such in John 19, after the soldiers have placed a crown of thorns on His head and a robe around His shoulders. He brings Jesus out to the people and Pilate says, "Here is the man!" (v. 5). This is the man, the One who all the Old Testament proclaims and the One who Daniel 7 reveals. He is man—having taken on flesh—but He is also God, possessing all dominion and glory and worthy of all worship. This is the Man, the new picture of what humanity is to be. We are not meant to be molded into the image of Adam, the first man, but into the image of Christ, the second, better Man, our new representative, the inaugurator of a new and better covenant. This is the Man who would suffer and die for His covenant people, not the first man who would bring forth suffering and death for his people. He is the Son of Man who has come to save us from ourselves, from our brokenness as those descended from Adam. Instead, He has come to exchange His life for ours so we may also be redeemed from being sons of Adam to being sons of God. And this kingdom that He rules, He rules from weakness as the Son of Man, crucified for us. As scholars of old have said, He was reigning even from the cross, because in weakness He has redeemed us all.[25]

The Son of Man has ruled from weakness, so that we who are weak may be made strong. He has become flesh so that we might be made like Him—the great exchange.

ADDITIONAL READING: Psalm 8:4; Matthew 24:29–31; Matthew 25:31; Hebrews 2:6; Revelation 14:14

GOOD NEWS OF GREAT JOY

But the angel said to them, "Don't be afraid, for look,
I proclaim to you good news of great joy that will be
for all the people: Today in the city of David a Savior
was born for you, who is the Messiah, the Lord."
Luke 2:10–11

The little cherubs resting on clouds in the now vintage painting in my childhood home are far from the obviously terrifying beings who appeared to the shepherds in the fields that night. This night was like the thousands before it for these shepherds, seeing only by the dim light of the moon and stars, guiding and protecting their sheep from the predators that roam in the night. That is, like the thousands before it until it wasn't.

The glory of the Lord shone around these angelic messengers, and after announcing this baby in a manger, a multitude of them appeared, glorifying God in a loud voice, "Glory to God in the highest heaven, and peace on earth to people he favors!" (v. 14). Can you even imagine the adrenaline? The good news of the Messiah—the One God's people had waited on and looked for across centuries was here, and His birth wasn't announced to the powerful and the rich. Instead, the humble and lowly were the recipients of this glorious goodness: the announcement that Good—it's source and its fullness—had come to earth in flesh. This baby, laid in a manger, is the Messiah, the Savior.

Yet it is not just the birth of Jesus that is good news to the listener. The goodness of God is found in all of who Jesus is: God Himself who took on our broken humanity so He could heal it from within, living the perfectly obedient life in our place and dying the substitutionary death we deserved for our sin, rising victorious over the sin and death that plagues us, and ascending to the right hand of the Father. This is the essence of Good; the long-awaited Savior is here, but He is far better than anyone imagined. Not only is He the Savior, He is God, who left the glory of heaven to take on flesh, in unbelievable humility, choosing to take on the infirmities of the flesh—in both body and mind.

God's redemption has arrived, revealing God in a language we can understand: flesh. He unleashed the goodness of God in a new way in the One who is Good: Jesus Christ. He was conceived by the Holy Spirit, born of the virgin Mary in miraculous goodness. He revealed to us God's good plan to bring heaven to earth and reconciliation to His people both with God and with One another.

Good news of great joy was not just for a moment in a field with some men responsible for the lives of a flock of (likely stinky) sheep. God Himself intervened in time and space and nothing would ever be as it was before. A taste of His goodness had come, and once you've truly tasted and seen that the Lord is good (Ps. 34:8), you cannot help but be drawn to Him, to the glory of His goodness.

What is goodness? It is Jesus. Is what you are facing good? Well, is Jesus in it? Does it bring great joy and glory to God in the highest heaven? Our highest good is not found in achievement or worldly glory, but in glory to God. Our highest good is not in health or wealth or status, it is in becoming like these shepherds, lowly, but with eyes that have seen where heaven meets earth and ears that have heard the glorious goodness of God: "a Savior is born for you, who is the Messiah, the Lord." He is our good. God has descended to earth so that we may know Him rightly, and from this comes all of our good. We know light because we know the Light of Lights. We know love because we know the One who is Love. We know what is good because God is the definition of good, and we see it clearly in Jesus, who as a baby in a manger is the Sustainer and Ruler of all the world. It's with this truth in mind that we read all the Scriptures. They are all about Him anyway. We begin with Christ because He is our good, but also because He is the center point of our faith, the One on whom it hinges. The good news is Jesus and His life, death, resurrection, and ascension that was completed for you, securing your reconciliation to God. This is good. Our good. Good is a Person.

ADDITIONAL READING: Exodus 34:6–7; Psalm 35:1–9; Romans 3:1–4

MY EYES HAVE SEEN
YOUR SALVATION

Now, Master,
you can dismiss your servant in peace,
as you promised.
For my eyes have seen your salvation.
You have prepared it
in the presence of all peoples—
a light for revelation to the Gentiles
sand glory to your people Israel.
Luke 2:29–32

Simeon lived the last years of his life waiting to see the Lord's promised Messiah with his own eyes. The Spirit was upon him, and Luke 2:25 says he "was righteous and devout, looking forward to Israel's consolation." The Spirit had revealed that he would not see death before he saw Jesus. Imagine the Spirit telling Simeon, "Alright. Today's the day!" The Scriptures say that he was guided by the Spirit to enter the temple, and then as Mary and Joseph approach, he sees the One he already loves and the One he has committed his life to serving.

He proclaims what I'm sure shocked Mary and Joseph, this baby before him is the salvation of God, prepared over centuries before people who saw glimpses of His light, but now in His fullness. This salvation wasn't only the completion of the promised covenant with Israel, but also the fulfillment of His call for Israel to be a light to the nations. The One who is God's Elect—His Chosen One—became that light to the nations when Israel had failed to do so, not as a response to their failure, but because God had always planned it to be that way. Jesus was the revelation of God that Israel could not be despite their interaction with Him because Jesus is God Himself. He's not "sorta God" or "a picture of God who we can't see." He is the fullness of the Godhead among us; not simply a picture of what God is like, but God Himself. Jesus is not a window we look through to the true and better God. He is not a conduit to a salvation found elsewhere—whether that be in the Father alone or in some other conception of God. He is God and He is salvation, and to look upon Him is to find it. Simeon knew this: "For my eyes have seen your salvation" (v. 30).

We've spent a lot of time focusing on Jesus's incarnation throughout these pages, and that is by design. There is no more important doctrine, no truer theology without Him. If Jesus is the revelation of God, then we cannot talk about what God has revealed without talking about the One who revealed it, the One who is God, coming to correct our knowledge of God and draw out our love for God. And here He is, just days old among a bustling temple. Other babies are also crying, people are talking and moving around, the temple looks like an anthill that has been stirred because so many are still in town for the annual feasts and census. He comes in unassuming and humble, not drawing a crowd.

The Spirit revealed the identity of this baby to Simeon, and he rejoiced, knowing he had seen the face of God. Mary and Joseph were amazed at what he said, especially as he continued: "Indeed, this child is destined to cause the fall and rise of many in Israel and to be a sign that will be opposed—and a sword will pierce your own soul—that the thoughts of many hearts may be revealed" (vv. 34–35). What terrifying truth this must have been! This tiny, precious baby would bring a sword among people; with His razor-sharp discernment, He would separate the wheat from the chaff even within our own soul, piercing even beyond joint and marrow (Heb. 4:12–13).

The gospel is good news to those who know they are perishing, but it is only worthy of disgust for those who wrongly believe they are fully alive, knowing neither Christ nor His grace. It is not the well who need a doctor, but the sick (Mark 2:17), and this doctor has the steadiest hand with a scalpel ready to cut away what does not flourish, to remove whatever pieces are decaying so that, as a whole, we may live despite it. He has brought a sword, a scalpel, that also separates family members and friends. The gospel is offensive to those who believe they have no need, to those who are appalled that God might pierce our hearts so that we may better know and love Him. The Revelation of God is also the means of the revelation of our soul, laying bare what is truly at the root of our affections. This raw transparency is painful but good, reminding us of our dire need for salvation and the fact that it only comes by way of Christ, a baby brought into a busy temple immediately recognized by the faithful of God, while year after year would pass in His life without recognition by those who claimed faithfulness but were far from Him. Our light, our glory has come, bringing salvation in His nail-scarred hands. What Simeon knew immediately we now also know. Jesus is salvation's destination, its path, and its prize because salvation is a Person.

ADDITIONAL READING: Psalm 37:39; John 14:6; Acts 4:12; 1 Peter 1:8–9

WHO DO PEOPLE
SAY THAT I AM?

When Jesus came to the region of Caesarea Philippi, he asked
his disciples, "Who do people say that the Son of Man is?"
They replied, "Some say John the Baptist; others, Elijah;
still others, Jeremiah or one of the prophets."
"But you," he asked them, "who do you say that I am?"
Simon Peter answered, "You are the Messiah,
the Son of the living God."
Matthew 16:13–16

I just get Peter. He's impulsive and so obviously flawed. He so dearly loves his friend Jesus (and so deeply misunderstands His purpose) that when Jesus is being arrested, Peter cuts off a guy's ear, and then Jesus miraculously puts it back on immediately. Imagine that conversation! Yet, even after seeing this and many other miracles, Peter is terrified after Jesus's crucifixion, denying that he even knew his beloved friend. Peter's humanity is endearing. And yet, this is the one on whom the church would be built: the struggler, the scared, the unlikely.

Just before this passage in Matthew 16, we get a glimpse into what the disciples do—or do not—understand about Jesus's teaching. Jesus warned them not to be deceived by the leaven of the Pharisees and Sadducees, and of course, they immediately start talking about bread rather than their teachings. This seemingly easy concept went over their head, tipping us off as readers that the even deeper question Jesus was about to ask likely wasn't fully understood either. Certainly so, as we see what happens with the disciples after the crucifixion. Yet, in what may be childlike faith, when asked, "Who do you say that I am?" Peter replies, "You are the Messiah, the Son of the living God" (vv. 15–16).

Don't let the familiarity be lost on you. Here, Peter is proclaiming just what Jesus has said about Himself: that He is the Messiah the Old Testament exalts. Jesus is the Second Adam, the faithful One. He is the "man [who] leaves his father and mother and bonds with his wife, and they become one flesh" (Gen. 2:24) and the crusher of the serpent's head (Gen. 3:15). He is God's Messiah, the Savior who would redeem God's people from oppression, not by means of a temporary earthly scepter, but in His eternal kingdom.

But Peter wasn't just calling Jesus God's Messiah, he called Him God's Son. To be God's Son is to be One with the Father. Peter is celebrating what we praise today: Jesus is God, but also man, able to redeem and reconcile us precisely because He is fully both. He is not the return of a prophet of the past, but God doing a new thing while also completing an old thing already in motion; entering space and time while also being already victorious, achieving salvation for us before time began (Heb. 4:3). In His abundant grace, God has given us salvation through the Son made flesh, the Messiah.

He intervened in our most desperate of situations; when we were lifeless and without hope, He laid His life down so that ours may be filled. Our salvation is not a nebulous thing that happens to us or in us. Our salvation is a Person.

What hung from the tree of the knowledge of good and evil was the curse, but the One who hung from the tree constructed into the shape of a cross was made the curse for us. As Pilate declares:, "Here is the man!" (John 19:5), the man from the beginning, the Second Adam. There is the man back in the beginning who brought about death, but here is the man who has come to be what the first man could not. Here is the man who will take away the sins of the world. The fruit of the first tree was poison, but the fruit of the second tree is unending life. This is the great exchange: a life for all lives that would trust Him; a death to end death itself. Our salvation is Christ Himself. He is both the conduit of our salvation and the prize. He was to be called Jesus because He will save His people from their sins, the fulfillment of His name which means "the Lord is salvation."

He truly is just as Peter said and we know even more deeply today: "the Messiah, the Son of the living God" (Matt. 16:16). Take a moment to reflect on the magnitude of the gift of salvation He has secured for you today. Your salvation was not an easy achievement, but it most certainly was a praiseworthy one.

ADDITIONAL READING: Psalm 68:19; Psalm 79:9; Luke 2:29–32; John 14:6; Acts 4:12

THE WAY

Jesus told him, "I am the way, the truth, and the life. No one comes to the Father except through me. If you know me, you will also know my Father. From now on you do know him and have seen him."
John 14:6–7

I have the directional ability of a toddler. My final year of college I used a GPS to find my house for more than six weeks after moving in. And in my worst "How on earth did I get here?" moment, I found myself headed to a retreat that was *not* on an island when my GPS announced: "Proceed to ferry." To navigate the world, we must have a good, trustworthy guide. But even with a good map, there are times user error has led me onto a floating parking lot, slowly drifting across a bay in the Gulf of Mexico.

A wrong turn here or there lands us far from where we intend to be. There's a particular way that leads to your destination. For the way that leads to life, there is a singular route: united into Christ through His life, death, resurrection, and ascension. The only One holy enough to be eternally with God is God Himself, so God the Son took on flesh so that we may be united in His humanity, imbued with His righteousness, gifted with His standing before God and His status as son and heir. We are in Christ and with Christ, through the work of Christ. He is the way. The holy One in whom we may also be made holy before God.

When we couldn't ascend to God, He descended to us. When we couldn't find a way, He didn't simply make a way or illuminate the way for us. He became the way. When we inherited sin from Adam, unable to do anything about it on our own, He lived the righteous life we couldn't live. He had no sin, inherited or committed. He stood in our place so that we might stand before God without blemish, just like Him, by being united in His life.

He is not one of many ways to a life with God, He is the *only* way. The God of the Bible is not Allah of the Qur'an or simply the force behind those who seem to be "good people." The narrow way is truly narrow, only available through the life, death, resurrection, and ascension of Jesus. No one comes to the Father except through Him. It's a winding path full of boulders to climb and underbrush to work through because not many walk it, but the view at the top is Christ, and there is no better view. The struggle through Leviticus (and other books very much removed from our culture), the struggle to unceasingly pray, the struggle to live rightly—it is a battle until the moment we see Him face-to-face, but it is worth it because of the coming view.

This way is not a geographical location or the blue dot traveling on a GPS screen. Instead, this path is a Person. He is the way back to a fruitful, loving relationship with our triune God. This is why we must know who it is we follow. If we do not know the One we serve, we won't recognize the right (or the wrong) path by its contours. Instead, we may follow a path to a dead end, only to realize we took the wrong side of the fork many miles earlier. Yes, we can return and correct our path, but it's difficult.

Know the One who is the path so you don't have to backtrack. His death is the image of the way to freedom from the sin that ensnares us, and

His resurrection is both the image of our new life in Christ and the promise of what is to come for those who believe and walk in the Way.

There is no other way to the Father. All roads are not equal. The way to life is narrow, but the way to death is wide and easy. He is the way of promise, the one who brings His people back from exile. The only way to true, lasting life. This place is not your home, but He has gone ahead to prepare a place for you, and the way is paved with faith in Christ and obedience to His Word. It is narrow, but it is worth it.

His way is life. To walk as He walked is to be a life-giver—a light—to all around you so that they, too, may know Him as the way. Are you traveling the narrow way? What areas of your life might need a U-turn today?

ADDITIONAL READING: Isaiah 44:6; Matt. 11:27; John 1:18; 1 John 5:11–12; Hebrews 9:11–12

THE TRUTH

Then Jesus said to the Jews who had believed him, "If
you continue in my word, you really are my disciples. You
will know the truth, and the truth will set you free."
John 8:31–32

As a child, my grandfather convinced me that chickens were baby eagles just waiting to grow into their full glory. I often chose to eat a hamburger instead of chicken nuggets as a child because I didn't want to harm baby eagles, robbing them from becoming what they were deemed to become.

What we believe is true holds bearing on our lives. Our theology drives our view of how we should treat our family and our neighbors, informs how we think about politics and serving our communities, and determines what we should believe is true about how we (and those around us) are designed. According to data completed by Dr. Fred Luskin at Stanford University, our brains think 90 percent of the same thoughts today that they thought yesterday.[26] Our brains return to what they know, and knowing the truth determines whether this spiral is toward or away from Christ. So how do we know the truth? How do you know you aren't watching for proverbial chickens to grow into eagles?

In a world of conspiracy theories, living your truth, and placebos, truth feels slippery and aloof. Yet the Truth isn't subjective or changing with trends because the Truth is a Person. Truth is Jesus. It is not a set of well-prepared statements to remember or memorize. Knowing the Truth is knowing God, who is all truth and all wisdom. This is the Ttruth that will set us free, because to know God is to trust Jesus for salvation, enjoying the freedom He gives from the chains of sin. We know Him because He has taken on flesh and we see Him in the pages of Scripture. God hasn't simply told us the truth, He sent us the Truth, forever joining heaven and earth. In John 8:31–32, Jesus encourages His followers to continue in His Word, which comes after a dispute about who Jesus is. He explained that He is from above, claiming God to be His Father. Those listening certainly did not understand, but we get to stand on the side of history that does understand. Jesus is the Truth, the revelation of God to us.

Katherine Sondregger makes a distinction between fact and truth in her chapter in *Christology: Ancient and Modern*. She says, "Truth, to speak in this ancient way, is more substantial, more exalted and transcendent" than what is known by scholastic work.[27] Truth is more true than facts. So, what is truly true about our reality in Christ? John points to Jesus as the Word made flesh (John 1) and to Jesus's I AM statements throughout His argument for Jesus as the One who is the Truth. This is the Truth that we proclaim—the Truth that shapes our every moment:

"I am the bread of life." (John 6:35)

"I am the light of the world." (John 8:12)

"I am the gate." (John 10:7)

"I am the good shepherd." (John 10:11, 14)

"I am the resurrection and the life." (John 11:25)

"I am the way, the truth, and the life." (John 14:6)

"I am the true vine." (John 15:1)

This is the Truth that sets us free, but also the Truth that is "foolishness to those who are perishing" (1 Cor. 1:18). So do you have questions about how to live, how to think, or how to trust God? Look at Jesus. He has come to redeem His people wholly—mind, body, and spirit—redeeming their minds to be able to understand and trust His truth, their bodies in the resurrection to never again be subject to decay or death, and their spirit so that it might be made one with Christ, worshipping Him forever.

The world's "truths" are loud, while the Spirit whispers the Truth, but don't mistake the quiet for weakness. It is a quiet power. The truth of the gospel is the only truth with the explosive power to save! The church father Augustine says it this way in his work *City of God*: "But it must not be supposed that folly is as powerful as truth, just because it can, if it likes, shout louder and longer than truth."[28]

What lies has the Enemy shouted at you, seeking to entice you to believe them? How might you return to the truest Truth, the gospel of Jesus Christ, today?

God, help us know and meditate on Your Truth. Give us
discernment and help us keep our minds on Christ.

ADDITIONAL READING: 1 Samuel 15:29; Psalm 86:11; John 1:17; John 8:32; John 14:6; 1 John 5:20

THE LIFE

Jesus said to her, "I am the resurrection and the life.
The one who believes in me, even if he dies, will live."
John 11:25

God brings life from the void and formless—light from the darkness. From the dust of the ground—that which would not host life—God fashioned man, a sort of resurrection even in the beginning bringing life from death. Even the garden of Eden springs forth from the ground after God planted it (Gen. 2:8–9), a process that only happens after a seed is impacted into the soil as if in a tomb, rotting before a sprout emerges from the cracked outer shell. God brings His people to the edge of the Jordan and then through its waters, a picture of the boundary between their past life and their new one in the Promised Land, moving them from a wilderness of death to a Promised Land beaming with life. The Old Testament consistently creates a longing for true, abundant life as the Israelites experience suffering, decay, and death again and again.

In Genesis 3, Adam and Eve faced immediate spiritual death—removal of the Breath of God that brought union with Him in the garden—and exile into the vast, uncultivated wilderness. And we inherit their brokenness as those who share in their humanity. Adam and Eve didn't need God to simply bring them back to the Garden or remove the physical distance created between them and God by their sin. They needed to be resurrected because they were spiritually dead, unable to respond to God's movement in their own strength. With the entrance of sin came a reign of death (Rom. 5:14). The world was bent toward it, growing toward the darkness instead of toward the light.

We are incapable of cultivating true life outside of Christ: a world intent upon death, crumbling under our feet. Yet Romans 5:17–19 brings great hope: "If by the one man's trespass, death reigned through that one man, how much more will those who receive the overflow of grace and the gift of righteousness reign in life through the one man, Jesus Christ. So then, as through one trespass there is condemnation for everyone, so also through one righteous act there is justification leading to life for everyone. For just as through one man's disobedience the many were made sinners, so also through the one man's obedience the many will be made righteous." Jesus Himself is our life. When we trust Him, the Holy Spirit unites us with Him—uniting us to the One who is abundant, eternal life. In Him, we have lived the perfectly obedient life because He has. In Him, we have died to sin with Him, and in Him, His resurrection reigns in our lives, having passed through the proverbial waters of baptism into His body. You await a resurrection in the pattern of Christ's, as 1 Corinthians 15 tells us, but you also have already been resurrected. You are already living your resurrected, eternal life. It doesn't begin when your body breathes its last. It begins when your soul breathes its first, when the breath of God that was lost in the garden enters in at your moment of surrender to His pursuing.

If you are in Christ, sin has no hold on you. You have died to it. Do not return to a life of death. Do not dwell among the spiritual catacombs, embracing the decay and stench of death that comes with our willful determination to sin. Instead, live in the light. Live as the one who has been made new because that is your truest self. You are "dead to sin and alive to God in Christ Jesus" (Rom. 6:11). And this is good news because, while death entered through Adam, life abounds and flourishes in Christ.

Jesus Himself is life. Every other path leads to sure death. In a world full of darkness and death, we are people of light and life. How are you being light today?

ADDITIONAL READING: Ezekiel 33:11; John 3:16; Romans 6:10–14, 22–23; Colossians 3:4

HE TOOK ON FLESH; MAN AMONG US

The Word became flesh and dwelt among us. We
observed his glory, the glory as the one and only Son
from the Father, full of grace and truth.
John 1:14

What is the center point of the Christian life? Most would say the cross because it secured our salvation, and I believe this is true, but it is also lacking. It isn't *just* the cross. The true center point of our faith is not a moment in the life of Christ, but the whole of it. Our salvation rests on the fullness of the incarnation—from the Son taking on our broken humanity, to the perfectly obedient life He lived, to His death on the cross, to His resurrection, and His ascension. If you are a Christian, you are united to Jesus, not just in His crucifixion, but in His whole life, vicariously lived for you.

God Himself became flesh and even suffered death, experiencing in His humanity what we experience. As the Second Adam, Jesus did in His humanity what Adam could not do because of his immaturity. Jesus is the perfectly mature, the infinitely wise, able to not just take on the difficulties and infirmities of our bodies, but to heal them from the inside out. Worthy of repeating from earlier is this from Gregory of Nazianzus, who lived from AD 329–397: "For that which He has not assumed He has not healed; but that which is united to His Godhead is also saved."[29] If He did not take on true human nature, He would not have healed it in His incarnation, but He did just that. He wasn't God who just looked like man but didn't really face life as we do, and He wasn't mostly God with just a little bit of man, as if the divine overwhelmed the humanity, which was barely existent.

No, this is the glory of the kindness of God: that He would stoop down so low, taking on our brokenness so that in Him, we might be made whole. He lived the perfectly obedient life in His humanity, redeeming what was lost in the garden as He chose to obey in another. As drops of blood fell from His brow in the garden of Gethsemane, Jesus chose to obey, even when it meant embracing human death, an obedience that Adam couldn't aspire to in his lack.

Jesus faced temptation and suffering to a degree that we will never face, because He shouldered the brokenness of all of humanity in His life and death. In His humanity, He has shown us what true humanity really is, because He is the mature, wise human. This humanity is embodied, humble, and walking in communion with God, and because our communion was so broken by corruption and guilt, God Himself provided the way for our humanity to be made right.

We don't trust God so that we can one day escape our humanity, as if our bodies are the problem. We trust God because only He can redeem us to humanity's original design: the pattern of Christ. He took on the death and degradation of sin in Himself, God made flesh. The Son, through whom all the world was made, and the stars continue to hold in their place (Col. 1:16–17), was born as a baby, reliant upon His earthly parents to provide for the needs of His little body. The baby in the manger was the most human human, unscathed by sin. "He is the image of the invisible God" (v. 15), but not only the image. He *is* fully God and fully man.

Without this truth, we would have no gospel, no salvation. Without Jesus's incarnation, we would not know God as we know Him now because Jesus revealed Him. He lived the life in flesh that we could not live, the rightfully human life of perfect obedience to God in full communion with Him. Jesus's crucifixion, resurrection, and ascension are glorious, making clear God has made us right through His blood, but the incarnation is not less important to our salvation and our understanding of the grace Jesus achieved. God Himself became one with flesh. He became like us in all of humanity's woes, healing them from the inside out. God united with humanity, Creator with creation so that we might truly know Him. We are united to Him in His body, participating with Him in His life, death, resurrection, and ascension.

Because we talk about the incarnation so often, we forget the glory of it—the unfathomable goodness of God that He didn't send us a set of instructions or write a message in the sky. He sent us His Son, the most beautiful of Messengers; a Messenger who understands us completely because He has lived just as we do. He understands what you face and He knows your struggles because He faced them too. Your Savior didn't just secure your salvation; He walked where you walk, and He advocates before the Father for you as One who gets it. And He is making you more and more truly human as He makes you more like Him. God has come and God will come again, and He did not just come to visit. He came to stay. He came to be like us so that we might become like Him.

ADDITIONAL READING: Isaiah 7:14; 2 Samuel 7:12–13; John 1:1, 14; Romans 8:3–4; 1 Timothy 3:16; Hebrews 2:14

HE TOOK ON FLESH;
GOD AMONG US

For the entire fullness of God's nature dwells bodily in Christ.
Colossians 2:9

The entire fullness. Let that sink in.

God revealed His fullness in the Son made flesh, the fullness of the One who created all things, delivered the Israelites out of Egypt, and orchestrated priests, judges, kings, and prophets. The One who made the sun stand still and who met with and disciplined His people. The One who proved to be faithful again and again and who is the source and substance of love, joy, peace, patience, kindness, goodness, faithfulness, gentleness, and self-control, cultivating them in the world and in our hearts through the Spirit. This is God, and in Christ, His fullness dwells—fully God and fully man.

While God sent angel messengers from time to time, this was a job He would achieve Himself, uniting the Godhead with broken humanity. God did what only God could do: provide a way to be right with Himself. He is both Creator and Corrector, providing remedy for our disobedience through His perfect obedience. He was conceived by the Holy Spirit, not by man, and He often proved it.

Jesus revealed His divine knowledge as He spoke with Pharisees, knowing what they were thinking (Matt. 12:25), and His power over all things as He turned water to wine (John 2:1–11) and healed the sick (Matt. 4:23). Jesus made the lame walk (John 5), the blind see (John 9), and the dead live (Luke 8:49–56, John 11). As amazing as these miracles are, the more unbelievable thing is what He often said to the one He had just healed, "Your sins are forgiven." No human had the authority to forgive sin, because the only One who can forgive an offense is the offended. Everyone in Jesus's day knew that even the high priest in the temple did not have the authority to pay for sin. Only God Himself could do that.

Yet Jesus is God, and He both forgives sin and atones for it. The sacrifices made to God would no longer be necessary in the temple because God Himself became the sacrifice as both the High Priest and even the Temple itself. He is the One on whom these systems and places of the Old Testament were built, to foreshadow on earth what was true in eternity. And when we are united in Him through faith, we are declared righteous by His sacrifice, elevated as citizens in a kingdom of priests who are always welcomed into His presence because we are His dwelling place, His temple. Through Jesus, we have direct access to God because we are united to Him in His humanity, and He is united to the triune God in His divinity.

Jesus is not two persons—one divine and one human—in a single body, and He is not one person operating in two personalities. He is fully God and fully man, two natures perfectly united together (called the hypostatic union). And all this so that we could be united to God, know Him rightly, and the debt we owed for our sin could be paid. He is God and He is good. God Himself came to dwell among people, conceived in the virgin womb of Mary, betrothed to Joseph, and laid to rest in the virgin tomb of Joseph of Arimathea. God became man so that we might know Him in His birth, life, death, resurrection, and ascension. He is the revelation of God because He *is* God.

Spend a moment thinking on this quote from Ignatius, an early church father:

> But our Physician is the only true God, the unbegotten and unapproachable, the Lord of all, the Father and Begetter of the only-begotten Son. We have also as a Physician the Lord our God, Jesus the Christ, the only-begotten Son and Word, before time began, but who afterwards became also man, of Mary the virgin. For "the Word was made flesh." Being incorporeal, He was in the body; being impassible, He was in a passible body; being immortal, He was in a mortal body; being life, He became subject to corruption, that He might free our souls from death and corruption, and heal them, and might restore them to health, when they were diseased with ungodliness and wicked lusts.[30]

ADDITIONAL READING: Isaiah 9:6; John 8:58; 10:30; 1 Corinthians 8:6; Hebrews 1:8

HE TOOK ON FLESH; HUMBLING HIMSELF

Adopt the same attitude as that of Christ Jesus,
who, existing in the form of God,
did not consider equality with God
as something to be exploited.
Instead he emptied himself
by assuming the form of a servant,
taking on the likeness of humanity.
And when he had come as a man,
he humbled himself by becoming obedient
to the point of death—
even to death on a cross.
Philippians 2:5–8

The Son of God, who is the agent of creation and one with the Father and Spirit, humbled Himself to the point of death on the cross, stripped naked and stapled to a tree, lifted high so He could be the sport of spectators. The glorious King of all took on flesh in the greatest act of humility, the incarnation.

He obeyed the Father in both life and death, deeming Himself nothing so that He could bring all glory to the Father, submitting completely to Him. He emptied Himself of His majesty and glory, His unlimited riches in the heavenly places. He didn't empty Himself of His deity; He is and was always God, even when He was laid in a borrowed manger in the town of David, far from His family's home. He did not stop being God, but He did humble Himself, taking on flesh and the woes and limits of a body. He did not demand obedience or worship; instead, He was meek and gentle, humbly yielding to the Father at every turn.

This is the attitude of Christ; the primary characteristic of His life: humility. Andrew Murray describes the many verses throughout John that proclaim his humility, like John 8:50 that says, "I do not seek my own glory . . ." Murray says, "They teach us what the essential nature and life is, of the redemption which Christ accomplished and now communicates. It is this: He was nothing that God might be all. He resigned Himself with His will and His powers entirely for the Father to work in Him. Of His own power, His own will, and His own glory, of His whole mission with all His works and His teaching, of all this He said, It is not I: I am nothing; I have given Myself to the Father to work; I am nothing, the Father is all."[31]

If only we would be so quick to yield to the Father's direction. As those being molded into the image of Christ, His humility is primary. Pride is at the root of all evil, and it is the reason the Enemy fell from grace. He sought to be greater than God, which is the same idea he fed Eve. Pride is our downfall, but humility our crown. Because in the living of a humble life, we get to echo the life of Christ, yielding to the Father who is worthy of all praise. This is the call of the Christian: come and die. We have to know what we are signing up for. We view ourselves as nothing in view of God's mercies, suffering with Christ and taking on His attitude of humility. A God who suffers would be unthinkable to the religious of Jesus's day, and yet He chose to take on suffering so that we might be made whole again, healed from our ultimate suffering at the hand of an Enemy who hates us.

He was meek and lowly, humble in all His ways. He didn't lord over anyone while on earth, despite being Lord over all. May we take on His attitude as those who have died and been raised with Him. How might you need to be humbled today?

ADDITIONAL READING: Isaiah 57:15; Luke 14:11; John 8:28; Hebrews 4:15

HE TOOK ON FLESH; EXALTED BY GOD

For this reason God highly exalted him
and gave him the name
that is above every name,
so that at the name of Jesus
every knee will bow—
in heaven and on earth
and under the earth—
and every tongue will confess
that Jesus Christ is Lord,
to the glory of God the Father.
Philippians 2:9–11

In May of 2023, one of the most watched moments in television history occurred: the coronation of King Charles III. I (and 20M of my closest friends) tuned in to see the king anointed with oil and crowned with the traditional St. Edward's crown made of solid gold. Then, his wife was also crowned, and they paraded from Westminster Abbey to Buckingham Palace in the fanciest 260-year-old carriage I've ever seen. Onlookers kneeled and cheered as he passed them by with much celebration. The coronation exalted the waiting king to his rightful throne, officially beginning his reign.

The poem Paul presents to us in Philippians 2:1–11 begins by highlighting the humility of Christ—His defining characteristic which singlehandedly qualifies Him for His rightful reign, while the second half coronates Him as King over all. With this exaltation comes a new reality: the era of the reign of Christ that is both already and not yet as we await its full reveal at the end of time. Whispers of His kingship are throughout His final week. Just before He enters Jerusalem He is anointed with costly perfume by Mary, in a sense, anointing Him as the King He already was but without fanfare or processional. Then, He's heralded like a king returning victorious from war as He rides into Jerusalem the Sunday before His crucifixion. People line the streets and shout "Hosanna!" as He passes. Yet He doesn't ride a majestic horse, but a small-for-Him donkey who has never been ridden, borrowed just for this occasion. I imagine His feet dragging the ground in what I'm sure was quite the spectacle. Even in His Triumphal Entry, His humility is evident.

In the moment of His greatest humility as He hung upon a cross, yielding to the plan of the Father, He was crowned with thorns and a sign was placed above His head sarcastically calling Him the "King of the Jews." I'd love to know what the man who wrote that sign would write today, because his sarcastic slur was not broad enough in its pronouncement. He would later reveal Himself to hundreds, including His closest companions, and then He would ascend into heaven to sit on His throne. He wasn't just the King of the Jews. He *is* King over all, and He reigns from heaven at the right hand of the Father. He is already reigning, but He also will one day banish sin, death, and the Enemy who seeks to only inflict harm on His beloved. He will right all wrongs as the good King that He is. We await the day when His Kingship is ushered in fully—when every knee will bow to His holy name and every tongue will confess, cheering for His kingdom reign.

While it may seem as though the world spins out of control and the Enemy is unfettered in His antics, the work has already been done. He will be defeated, and every knee will bow to the true King who hates what the Enemy has done to humanity. The Enemy's days are numbered, and it is in God's patient lovingkindness that He delays, so that all might hear and know the good news of the gospel. May we live like our King is on the throne. Because He is.

ADDITIONAL READING: Zechariah 9:9–10; Matthew 21:1–11; Acts 5:31; Ephesians 4:10; Revelation 5:12

THE GREAT HIGH PRIEST

*Therefore, since we have a great high priest who has ascended
into heaven, Jesus the Son of God, let us hold firmly to the faith
we profess. For we do not have a high priest who is unable to
empathize with our weaknesses, but we have one who has been
tempted in every way, just as we are—yet he did not sin. Let us
then approach God's throne of grace with confidence, so that we
may receive mercy and find grace to help us in our time of need.*
Hebrews 4:14–16 NIV

In the Old Testament, the high priest held the most important role in
the worship that happened in the tabernacle, and later, the temple. God
chose a family, the Levites, to lead Israel by teaching the Law, bringing offerings and gifts to the Lord, rightly ordering worship, and even declaring a
person clean or unclean. While the other tribes received portions of land,
God Himself was to be their portion. The high priest would enter the presence of God in the Holy of Holies once a year, and "never without blood"
(Heb. 9:7) for the covering of his own sin and the sins of the people.

God spoke both to and through his priests. They were a picture of
God to the people in their practice of holiness and authority, and more

importantly, they were an advocate for the people before God. They stood between God and man, reconciling the two through the offerings, though it was only temporary reconciliation through the covering of their sin by the blood of a sacrifice.

The priestly lineage and duties were a part of the stipulations of the Old Covenant, and with the New Covenant came a new priestly lineage with new duties. God the Son took on flesh, and with flesh He also took on the role of the Great High Priest for all who would trust Him. He became the offering giver and the offering itself, giving His life on the cross so that by His blood we might be reconciled with God. It is by His blood that we may enter His presence and be declared clean, as He is clean, free from the malignancy of sin and the stench of death that comes with it. The priests of the lineage of Levi could declare someone clean upon inspection, but Christ, as our High Priest, *makes* us clean through His blood.

While the Law contained many stipulations of how the clean might be made unclean by touching something dead or diseased or a number of other ways, Jesus could touch the unclean and make them clean, as we see in both those He healed and those He raised from the dead—often not just solving their malady, but forgiving their sin. This High Priest can empathize with us because He has walked in this world of suffering and trial, just as we have, and He has done so perfectly. This is the One who advocates for you as He sits at the right hand of the Father.

He is not a Mediator who does not understand what you are going through, but He is a perfect Mediator because He is both God and Man, sharing the mind of God and understanding the thoughts of humanity. If you trust Jesus, He has made atonement for your sin, and He has welcomed you in as a priest, giving you an assignment to serve in His kingdom too. You not only can enter into the Holy of Holies, but you *are* the Holy of Holies, the temple of God. All access is yours.

The Great High Priest has advocated for you, declaring you eternally clean. May we serve Him by proclaiming His glory so that others, too, might be declared clean by His sacrifice. You have an Advocate, and He is good. And this Advocate has made a way for you to approach God's throne of grace with confidence, knowing that God will always provide grace and mercy because you don't go to the throne alone. Your Advocate is with you, speaking to the Father about His blood that covers you. Approach Him with confidence today.

God, thank You for planning for a Great High Priest who could both make us clean and stand in our place before You. Thank You for counting His account when You look upon us. There is no good You withhold from Your Son, and no good You withhold from us on His account. We do not deserve a Mediator who would seek a righteous verdict for us, but You have done it out of Your goodness, despite our lack. God, thank You for this good gift. The blood of Your Son has covered our sin.

ADDITIONAL READING: Exodus 19:6; Psalm 110:4; Hebrews 2:17; Hebrews 7:11–28

THE RIGHT SACRIFICE

According to the law almost everything is purified with blood,
and without the shedding of blood there is no forgiveness.
Hebrews 9:22

B lood is the conduit for every cell in your body to receive what it needs to go on living. As Leviticus 17:11 says: "For the life of a creature is in the blood . . ." Blood is the life of the living—if there's no blood, there's no life. The amount of talk of blood in the Old Testament is enough to make any of us queasy, but these original hearers were intimately acquainted with blood. It was a necessary component in the covering of sin so that God's people could worship Him in the tabernacle or in the temple. It was sprinkled on God's people as a picture of the sealing of their covenant (Exod. 24:8) and present in the sign of the Old Covenant: circumcision (Gen. 17:11). It would be the sign of deliverance brushed above the doors of God's people when they were held captive in Egypt and the firstborn of every Egyptian household died, but the blood provided covering for the Israelite homes (Exod. 12:13–28).

The verse above continues: "For the life of a creature is in the blood, and I have appointed it to you to make atonement on the altar for your lives, since it is the lifeblood that makes atonement" (Lev. 17:11). Only life can pay for life. New life is only found through first, death. Romans 6:23 says: "For the wages of sin is death, but the gift of God is eternal life in Christ Jesus our Lord." If sin's right payment is death, the spilling of blood is the only covering strong enough to remove our sin.

The way that leads to death could only be covered by its necessary end: death. In the sacrificial system of the Old Testament, the life of the offering was exchanged for the life of the one bringing the offering. A life for a life. The innocent for the guilty. Blood spilt to atone for sin. Yet the blood of lambs and goats was not lasting. While their blood gave the people ritual cleansing, it could never provide cleansing for their hearts, so they had to bring offerings again and again. Only God could provide true cleansing, a work of the Spirit to produce fruit.

Jesus was unlike the sacrifices of the past. Jesus is both fully God and fully man, able to stand in humanity's place because He is one with us. He is and able to stand rightly before God because He is one with Him. God did what only God could do. He removed the need for the spilling of blood in the temple, which was both a constant and recurrent need for God's people, by spilling His own blood. His blood, poured out for us.

Praise the Lord! His blood is enough. We are wholly forgiven and completely reconciled to God, once and for all. He stood in our place so that we might have life—experiencing death and God's punishment for sin on our behalf. This is the good news of the gospel! Jesus's blood has paid the penalty for our sin, and as those covered in His blood, we are hidden from the burning glory of God. This is the glory that no man can see and live. As those united to Him, we have been delivered from the grip of sin and get to participate in the life of Christ. Our deliverance was costly: a life for a life. This is the extent God has gone to win you back to Himself. While the pain was great, His love was greater. His blood has purified us from our uncleanness, saving us so we might live both today and forever in God's wonderful presence.

> For you know that you were redeemed from your empty way
> of life inherited from your ancestors, not with perishable things
> like silver or gold, but with the precious blood of Christ, like
> that of an unblemished and spotless lamb. (1 Pet. 1:18–19)

ADDITIONAL READING: Isaiah 53:4–5; Romans 5:6–8; Hebrews 9:12–14

ALL THINGS HELD TOGETHER

He is the image of the invisible God,
the firstborn over all creation.
For everything was created by him,
in heaven and on earth,
the visible and the invisible,
whether thrones or dominions
or rulers or authorities—
all things have been created through him and for him.
He is before all things,
and by him all things hold together.
Colossians 1:15–17

All things are held together—not by your impressive organizational skills or your strategies, not by your work ethic or your wise intention, but by the Son who created it all. His careful hand both formed the sea and told it how far it is allowed to travel up the beach, both created the sun and set its distance from us. He designed gravitational pull, gave protons their charge, and set the speed of the earth's rotation, and even in this majesty, He also cares for you, one of more than eight billion people on earth. And He sustains each of them as well.

God has not only designed the world along with all its rules of physics and chemistry and biology, but He is the One who, moment-by-moment, day-by-day, holds all things together, spiritually, emotionally, and even physically. Gravity holds our feet to the earth at His command. He tells the earth to continue to move along its axis at the perfect speed and the perfect angle, and He instructs the atoms in the ways they should go; actively near and engaged to His creation even at the molecular level.

Through the Son, all things were created, and through Him all things continue. He provides your next breath, sustaining you, holding you in His love and holding you together. You weren't just created by Him, but also for Him, designed for His glory and His eternal kingdom. Your purpose is in Him because He determined it; your future is in Him because He planned it; your life is in Him because He holds it. He is actively sustaining the universe, while He actively sustains you. Hebrews 1:3 says: "The Son is the radiance of God's glory and the exact expression of his nature, sustaining all things by his powerful word." It is at His word that we "live and move and have our being" (Acts 17:28). He spoke, and all was created, and He speaks and all things are held together. The gentle hum of His voice rings forth in all of His works, testifying of Him.

His sustaining power isn't just something we try to meditate on so that we won't worry. It really is true. Through the Son, all things were created and all things hold together. When everything in your life feels like it is falling apart, when hard moment after hard moment comes and you can't seem to catch a break, your Savior is holding you together. He has given you His Word and He has given you His church—His body. As long as you remain in His body, you won't fall apart from it. God is with His church, the place of His presence and the outpost of heaven, and He holds it and you within it—all held perfectly together.

His power is unspeakable, that He might keep atoms together, our world spinning, and our feet on the ground. How much more will He sustain the ones He loves? How much more will He hold together the ones He laid His life down for? He sees and He knows, and He invites you to find comfort in Him when the world seems to spin out of control. Since before the dawn of creation, He has held it together; even before the day of your birth, He has done the same for you. He is holding you together.

ADDITIONAL READING: Acts 17:28; Romans 1:20–22; Hebrews 1:1–3

THE SNAKE CRUSHER

"I will put hostility between you and the woman,
and between your offspring and her offspring.
He will strike your head,
and you will strike his heel."
Genesis 3:15

The God of peace will soon crush Satan under your
feet. The grace of our Lord Jesus be with you.
Romans 16:20

Hostility. Opposition. This is the promise of life in this world where the Serpent continues to hold his temporary power. Paul calls him the "god of this age" (2 Cor. 4:4) and his reign is one of chaos and destruction. Ultimately, he is on a mission to bring about the stench of death into all of life. (It's notable that snakes have musk-producing glands, and the more venomous snakes are often thought to smell like rotting carcasses.) We should smell the Serpent coming who whispers to us the same lie he whispered to Eve, but all too often our senses are dulled by our complacency. Satan is excellent at convincing us that we should be comfortable and secure, and that because we love Jesus, we are somehow insulated from his attacks. That way, he can sneak up on us undetected and strike at just the right time when we are alone or weak.

A serpent was worn on the center of the headdress of Egyptian pharaohs as a symbol of leadership and power, and in many cultures, including the ancient gods of Greece, serpents were associated with wisdom. The deceitful Serpent in the garden sought to lure the woman by offering up what he claimed was true wisdom. He also is a ruler who knows he has no functional power, and he's clawing and scratching his way forward, hoping that he might gain some ground in the impossible fight against the sovereign rule of God. He's after your head, your mind, and your heart, hoping he can deceive you, which is his trick we've already seen play out in the garden. We know his aim is to steal, kill, and destroy; and we know his tactics. And while we don't succeed in pushing darkness back every time, we know the One who will. His seemingly most successful victories will look like embarrassing defeat in light of the glory of Jesus's victory over him. You may struggle with his tug-of-war for your affections and your ambitions. You may even stumble as he wraps around your leg, hoping you'll believe his whispers that try to convince you God doesn't really want what's best for you or that a life that glorifies Him isn't really worth the effort. He may strike your heel, but his days are numbered.

Even as God pronounced judgment upon the Serpent who would forever crawl on his belly, made to eat the dust of the ground in his moving about, He promised a Messiah who was to come. The Messiah is the only Wise One, the true Ruler of all. He is the snake raised upon the pole in the wilderness, bringing life to all who looked upon Him, while the other serpents who could only bring death, not life, struck at them (Numbers 21:4–9). He has broken the power of sin and death, and soon, He'll finish the job.

Satan's hold on the world would be strong, but it would be short. One would come who would crush the head of the Serpent, defeating the one with whom humanity has ultimate hostility and returning all things to peace. This work is not yet complete, but it has been firmly established in Christ's death, resurrection, and ascension, as Jesus descended to hell, defeating sin and death, and then rose as our victorious King. So we wait. We wait as those with hope and those who have the indwelling of the peace of God through the Spirit. We wait as those who know the end. And those who know that it is both globally and individually good.

There's a beautiful piece of art by Sr. Grace Remington called *Mary and Eve*. It depicts a serpent wrapped around Eve's leg while she meets with Mary, great with child. This is the Child who would crush the Serpent's head. Mary cradles Eve's downtrodden face, who seems to hold the sadness of a world spun into sin through her actions in her eyes, as though to say, "Just wait." Eve touches Mary's belly while clutching the devastating forbidden fruit to her chest, a picture of her great sin and the One who would take it all away. Spend some time reflecting on this piece of art and its message today.[32]

ADDITIONAL READING: Hebrews 2:14; James 4:7; 1 John 3:8; Revelation 12:9–10

47

LIVING WATER THAT BIRTHS A SPRING

Jesus said, "Everyone who drinks from this water will get thirsty again. But whoever drinks from the water that I will give him will never get thirsty again. In fact, the water I will give him will become a well of water springing up in him for eternal life."
John 4:13–14

Under the brutal heat of the desert sun, survival depends upon access to water, and death comes quickly for those who cannot find it. And yet, when Hagar finds herself deep in the barren wilderness sure of her own impending death due to the elements, God opens her eyes to see a full well of water (Gen. 21:19), in a place where a well was certainly uncommon.

When God's people wander in the desert for forty years and find themselves in a place with no water for the more than 600,000 people (Num. 1:46), God brings forth rushing water from a rock (Exod. 17:6; Num. 20:8–11). Can you imagine how much water would need to come from this rock to bring life-giving water to these people?

Throughout Scripture, weddings are arranged at wells, and water is offered by both stranger and friend for travelers and their animals. God describes Himself as the fountain of living water in Jeremiah 2:13, and the River of Life scattered across Scripture (see Ezek. 47; Rev. 22:1–2) are often descriptive of the Spirit's presence. Like the call to be a tree planted by streams of water (Ps. 1:3), there is no One that can provide the necessary water for all aspects of our life but God. Civilization has settled near flowing water since the beginning of time because flourishing only comes where water is present, and true flourishing that only God can bring is through His living water. This water quenches our eternal thirst for more—for something beyond today. Where a vast desert of extreme darkness and brutal sun, cold and heat, was once formed due to our transgressions, a rushing river has been formed, cutting through the wasteland of our broken lives and bringing with it flourishing of all kinds. The banks of this river overflow with fruiting trees, as the Spirit cultivates gifts and Christlikeness in our hearts.

If you are in Christ, trusting Him as the only living water in a dry and desert land, then in you is a stream of eternal life that cannot be dammed. It is a fountain of life for both you and for those around you, flowing from its source: the Giver of living water. He is the One who has sustained your life when your eyes were tricked by the oases of your mind, tempting you to believe another source of this water may exist somewhere else in the things of this world. He is the breath that fills our lungs with His songs, the living water that we drink so that we may partake in life with God, and the bread of life that we eat, so that we may be spiritually nourished—spiritually whole—through Him alone.

Put down your shovel and stop digging for worldly water that doesn't satisfy. Run to Jesus, who offers living water to all who need a drink.

ADDITIONAL READING: Psalm 36:9; Jeremiah 2:13; Zechariah 14:8–9; John 7:38; Revelation 21:6; 22:1–2

PREPARING FOR A WEDDING

Husbands, love your wives, just as Christ also loved the
church and gave Himself up for her, so that He might
sanctify her, having cleansed her by the washing of water
with the word, that He might present to Himself the church
in all her glory, having no spot or wrinkle or any such
thing; but that she would be holy and blameless. . . .
For this reason a man shall leave his father and his mother and be
joined to his wife, and the two shall become one flesh. This mystery
is great; but I am speaking with reference to Christ and the church.
Ephesians 5:25–27, 31–32

In the ancient Near East, weddings followed a months-long season of betrothal. Often, the groom's father (or a servant of the father) chose a bride for his son like Abraham does for Isaac in Genesis 24. After a bride was selected, the couple performs a betrothal ceremony. The betrothed man (or his father) pays the father of the bride the *mohar*, which is money, goods, or livestock given to the father of the bride in exchange for the opportunity to marry his daughter. Then, the awaiting new husband pours perfume over his new wife's head and gives her gifts[33] before they sign the ketubah, a marriage contract. While this makes them husband and wife, they do not live together or celebrate with a wedding ceremony until months later, after the new husband builds an acceptable dwelling for them.

After the husband finishes preparing a place for his wife, the husband and his friends dress in their special wedding clothing and approach the new wife's home, where she is waiting, but unaware of when her groom would arrive. She must be in a state of perpetual readiness. When her husband arrives with music and dancing, there would be days—often an entire week—of celebration. The couple often wore crowns on their heads during this huge party, signifying them as the guests of honor as they celebrated and feasted with their friends and family.

During this celebration, the marriage was consummated, making it "official official." This consummation wasn't primarily about sex, as it is so often portrayed to be in Western culture today. Instead, those in the ancient Near East viewed this consummation primarily as a personal self-disclosing, vulnerably allowing another to know you completely. Two made one, fully knowing one another.[34]

In Ephesians, Paul equates the mystery of union with Christ to that of a marriage into the known backdrop of these marriage practices. The separation of families, possessions, and living spaces is removed, and until death, the intention is that there will never again be a moment where this separation is reintroduced. This mysterious joining of two testifies to the truth of the gospel: the joining of those who trust Jesus to Him who are the church, resulting in the sharing of all His rights, privileges, and provisions. Betrothed now, awaiting the return of our Bridegroom, but already having the poured-out Spirit and "every spiritual blessing" (Eph. 1:3). He has gone to prepare a place for us, and when He returns, we will feast and celebrate eternally, fully knowing the One who has self-disclosed Himself to us.

The final verses are reminiscent of Genesis 2:24, arguably the first proclamation of the gospel message in the Scriptures: the man leaves his family and bonds with his wife. This is abnormal in all cultures; it is the wife that leaves her family and clings to the husband. The Son of God is the only groom who has left the communion of the Godhead to join to His wife, the church. While this passage in Ephesians does have a word for marriages, that is not the main point. His love is committed to our holiness, purifying us with His love and providing opportunity to trust Him in His sanctifying design.

Like a bride preparing herself for her groom, so the church waits for that day. And what a beautiful, glorious celebration this will be! And we will cast the crowns that have been placed on our heads at His feet.

> Let us be glad, rejoice, and give him glory,
> because the marriage of the Lamb has come,
> and his bride has prepared herself.
> (Rev. 19:7)

ADDITIONAL READING: Genesis 2:24; Matthew 25:1–13; Ephesians 5:22–33

THE FULFILLMENT
OF THE LAW

*"Don't think that I came to abolish the Law or the Prophets. I did
not come to abolish but to fulfill. For truly I tell you, until heaven
and earth pass away, not the smallest letter or one stroke of a letter
will pass away from the law until all things are accomplished."*
Matthew 5:17–18

The Israelites complained constantly in the wilderness, and even beyond
it. But they never complained about the Law despite its complexity.
The Law had always been the way of life for them, God's giving of His good
plan for their flourishing. They continually fell short of its limits, but it was
not disdained. They did not equate the reception of the law with a taking
away of their freedom, as we often do in the Western world. Instead, the
Law was a gift to them. Yet still, it was also an ideal far too great to achieve.
To obey God's Law led to life, while disobedience led to death. So God
provided a sacrificial system to trade a life for a life so that His people would
not suffer this consequence.

Jesus utters what is ultimately unintelligible to the Pharisee: "I did not
come to abolish but to fulfill" (v. 17). No one could fulfill the Law, at least

no one the Pharisees had met yet. The more than six hundred laws were complex and extensive, even the wisest person had been unable to keep it in totality. Yet, the One who is not only man but also God did. He did not need to be made right with God through sacrifice because He had not broken the Law, but also because He Himself is God. There was no need to become right with Himself. He was perfectly right in all of His ways.

Christ perfectly fulfilled the Law, so He had no debt to pay, no necessary offering to give. Instead, He became our sacrifice—a life for a life, but not like the lives of sheep or bulls, the life of the God-Man, the Son of God made flesh. God paid for the penalty of our sin to reconcile us to Himself. And in Christ, there is no longer any condemnation. Our inability to keep the Law no longer leads down the path to death because death no longer reigns. The Law and our ability to keep it is no longer our litmus for blessing or curse. Still, Jesus did not come to abolish the Law as if God no longer cared about holiness. He did not abolish it, as if God's way was no longer the way to flourishing and abundant life. Instead, God's people were given that life in full in Christ.

When we couldn't keep the Law, He took on flesh to keep it in our place. When we deserved condemnation, Jesus brought us innocence through the fulfillment of the Law on our behalf. When we could not ascend to God, He descended to us in flesh. Irenaeus, the church father, says it this way: "How is Christ the end of the Law if he is not also the final cause of it? For he who has brought in the end himself also made the beginning. And it is he who says to Moses, 'I have surely seen the affliction of my people who are in Egypt, and I have come down to deliver them' [Exod. 3:7–8]. It was customary from the beginning for the Word of God to ascend and descend for the purpose of saving those who were in affliction."[35]

This is the way of life: to walk with Christ, not to walk uprightly in regards to the Law, because we could not do it, but to trust the One who has, the One who is both the giver of the Law and its only fulfiller, the One who has both lived in holiness and shared His righteous account with us. Praise God! We are not under the Law, but under grace through the goodness of God made flesh.

Spend some time scanning through Leviticus today. Allow yourself to be overwhelmed by the amount of instructions it holds and moved to worship that God would send His Son to fulfill what we could not perfectly obey.

ADDITIONAL READING: Isaiah 42:21; Matthew 22:37–39; Luke 24:44; Romans 8:3–4

THE FULFILLMENT OF
THE PROPHETS

He told them, "These are my words that I spoke to you while
I was still with you—that everything written about me in the
Law of Moses, the Prophets, and the Psalms must be fulfilled."
Luke 24:44

Have you ever driven across the vast, seemingly never-ending reddish-brown dusty wilderness that is Texas? Imagine all that reddish-brown covered in silvery coins. Every inch of the state covered in two feet of silver dollars. That's roughly one hundred quadrillion silver dollars for those of us counting.

Now, a friend has marked one of those coins with an X and your job is to find it. Blindfolded. This is the statistical likelihood that a person would fulfill just eight of the more than three hundred prophecies about the coming Messiah in the pages of Scripture.[36]

Yet Luke is not only referencing the prophecies that proclaimed Jesus as Messiah, but the entire canon of the prophets' writings. Jesus doesn't just fulfill the promise of a baby born in Bethlehem (Mic. 5:2) who would end up in Egypt (Hosea 11:1), and whose ministry would begin in Galilee

(Isa. 9:1–2). He fulfilled every prophecy, and so many of them were not elements of a life that could be engineered. Statistically alone, it's more likely that Jesus is the Messiah than that He is not.

He fulfills the prophets' call for justice as the One who would bring true and eternal justice for the oppressed and peace for the afflicted. He is the good King over all the unrighteous kings who so often bore the weight of the prophet's declaration. He is the righteous Jonah, the One who obeyed God's call to go and proclaim the good news to a people destined for wrath. Jesus is not simply a messenger sent by God; He *is* God. He is the good Prophet, the Message of God's judgment and His provision—His call to repentance. He is not another prophet in a long line of prophets, but He is both the true and better Prophet, with Himself as the Message, the Gift, and the Giver. As Hebrews 1:1–2 says: "Long ago God spoke to our ancestors by the prophets at different times and in different ways. In these last days, he has spoken to us by his Son. God has appointed him heir of all things and made the universe through him."

Matthew went to great lengths to reveal Jesus as the Messiah in his Gospel, pointing to His fulfillment of the prophets. Nine different times across the Gospel of Matthew, he writes: "This was to fulfill . . . ," providing the particular prophecy that Jesus fulfilled, including being born of a virgin (Isa. 7:14 fulfilled in Matt. 1:22), brought up out of Egypt (Hosea 11:1 fulfilled in Matt. 2:17), and healing the sick (Isa. 53:4 fulfilled multiple times, Matt. 8:17 is one of them). Every word about Him rang true in His life, many of which were situations that a mere man could not intentionally arrange, like where and how He was born. The promised Messiah arrived in flesh millennia ago, and the evidence that He is to be trusted as such is overwhelming. God has done as He promised, and in Him we have the fulfillment of the Law, the Writings, and the Prophets. "For every one of God's promises is 'Yes' in him" (2 Cor. 1:20).

Spend time thanking God for the gift of the prophets so that we might know Jesus truly is the Messiah, the Son of God who came to bring us back from exile into His kingdom as His children and heirs through His blood. Praise God for His gift of fulfillment—that He has clearly proclaimed the truth of His Son throughout the Scripture and that, in His Son, we have deliverance from our deserved punishment through the One who has fulfilled the judgment of God for sin by taking it upon Himself. This is the good news of Jesus.

ADDITIONAL READING: Matthew 1:22; Matthew 2:15; Matthew 13:35; Acts 3:18; 2 Corinthians 1:20

51

THE FULFILLMENT OF
THE WRITINGS

It is from him that you are in Christ Jesus, who became wisdom
from God for us—our righteousness, sanctification, and redemption.
1 Corinthians 1:30

He told them, "These are my words that I spoke to you while
I was still with you—that everything written about me in the
Law of Moses, the Prophets, and the Psalms must be fulfilled."
Luke 24:44

In the Gospels, we meet a Savior—the Word made flesh—who quotes Psalms more than any other book of the Bible. He entered a religious scene hyper-focused on the Law and its required sacrifices, feasts, and festivals, and yet He didn't call people to a deeper obedience of the Law, but a deeper affection for God that drives people to the heart of not the Law, but the heart of the Law-Giver, with compassion, gentleness, truth, justice, and ultimately, wisdom. He intended that the source of their obedience be love, not duty.

Jesus made it clear He didn't only fulfill the Law's requirements—proclaiming innocence for His people through their union with Him and His perfect record—He also fulfills the writings, as the embodiment of what the writings call the reader to: wisdom. This wisdom is better than gold (Prov. 16:16) and worthy of pursuit (Prov. 4:1–13), because the one who finds it is blessed (Prov. 3:13), ultimately because the one who finds wisdom finds Christ, the One who embodies perfect wisdom.

He is the answer to the vanities of life that Solomon laments in Ecclesiastes and the answer to how to be always wise, never foolish in Proverbs. Not only is He the one with all wisdom, He *is* all wisdom, as 1 Corinthians 1:30 proclaims: "He became wisdom from God for us—our righteousness, sanctification, and redemption." It is in His wisdom that we might respond to His gift of salvation through the power of the Spirit. This is good news! He is both like us and so unlike us; perfect in wisdom, never engaging in folly.

I wish I could say the same of myself, and yet, like Paul, there are times when my knowledge doesn't match my life. As Paul says, "For I do not understand what I am doing, because I do not practice what I want to do, but I do what I hate" (Rom. 7:15). Even when I desire to do as God has instructed, I struggle to obey. Yet, Jesus didn't obey in His head alone, believing as He should and knowing right from wrong, which we often correlate with wisdom. True wisdom goes beyond knowledge into action. The writings don't reveal to us a wisdom of simple intellectual knowledge, but of commitment to response in everyday obedience. Walking in wisdom is to live as Jesus lived: the One who is wise. But this is not possible on our own. Walking in wisdom is only possible if we are walking with Jesus. He has fulfilled the writings as Wisdom Himself, and we, too, can be wise through His mediating for us and the guidance of the Spirit. The beginning of knowledge is the fear of the Lord (Prov. 1:7), but the beginning of wisdom is unity with Christ. Every wise truth in the writings is fulfilled in Him.

Every lament of Lamentations finds its comfort in Christ. Every vanity of Ecclesiastes finds purpose in Christ. Every psalm of praise finds its object in Christ. Every proverb of wise instruction finds its perfect example in Christ. Every proverb about the fool displays the life of the one disconnected from Christ. Every beauty in Song of Songs proclaims the beauty of the relationship of Christ to His church. Every needed comfort for Job can be found in Christ. Every book of history finds its conclusion in Christ. Every writing is fulfilled in Him.

The Bible is a single story, pointing to a Savior and His rightful victory over all as the One who has fulfilled the Law, the writings, and the prophets—the only One who could reveal true Wisdom. Ask the One who is Wisdom to give you wisdom today.

ADDITIONAL READING: Job 28:28; John 5:39; Colossians 2:2–3

THE FIRSTFRUITS OF
WHAT IS TO COME

But as it is, Christ has been raised from the dead, the firstfruits
of those who have fallen asleep. For since death came through a
man, the resurrection of the dead also comes through a man. For
just as in Adam all die, so also in Christ all will be made alive.
1 Corinthians 15:20–22

The offering of the firstfruits would occur once a year, just as the fields ripened (as instructed in Leviticus 23:9–16). Farmers brought the first of their crop into the temple to offer to God, proclaiming their trust in Him to finish His work of providing for them. While the farmers worked the soil and planted the seed, it was God who brought the rain and the growth. He caused the seed to rot, crack open, and bear life—a small seedling slowly inching its way out of the dirt as it sought the nourishment of the sun.

This offering wasn't only to testify to God's provision of the daily bread they needed through the fruit of their fields, though. Deuteronomy 26 calls the attention of the Israelites to the faithfulness of God to them as He delivered them out of Egypt with signs and wonders and into a land of milk and honey. In the kindness of God, He provided the beautiful, fertile land they

saw from across the Jordan for their possession. This was the land that pro-
duced the firstfruits for them.

Now, when farmers brought the first sheath of their fields' grain into
the temple, it wasn't a trip down the street. They were pilgrimaging all the
way back to the temple in Jerusalem, which lasted a week in the spring. The
offering took place the day after Passover, and it would become the marker
from which fifty days were counted to the celebration of Pentecost at the
end of the grain harvest.

The grain that grew in their fields was a provision from the Lord, but
this was a harvest that only results in sustenance for a city. Tomorrow comes
and they are hungry again. But what occurred on the day of the offering
of the firstfruits around AD 30 brought a provision that would far outlive
a season of harvest.[37] Jesus, the spotless Lamb, was slaughtered on a crimi-
nal's cross on the day of preparation for the Passover, historically the day
when a lamb was selected and prepared for the festival to commemorate
the Israelites' deliverance out of Egypt. The day after Pentecost, the day of
the firstfruits, is when He rose again. He is the one sheath of grain brought
before God as testimony that more of the same are to come. His resurrection
is the first of many, and all who trust Him are included in the crop of the
redeemed: those who will be resurrected with Him when He returns.

The seeds of faith are sown in our hearts, growing deep roots, awaiting the day we will bear the ultimate fruit of our salvation: resurrection.
Jesus has gone before us as the first. He defeated sin and death in the tomb,
and after, His body was raised, perfected and new, prepared for the New
Jerusalem where we will one day dwell with Him.

The resurrected body, unaffected by decay or sin, is not for Christ
alone, although no one else has yet participated in its glory. We will be like
Christ, raised from the dead and prepared for eternal life with Him. The
time between the firstfruits and the broader harvest is short. And Jesus is our
sure forerunner, gone to prepare a place for us. May He find us growing and

developing fruit as we await this harvest. You are His vine, His field. What fruit are you bearing?

ADDITIONAL READING: Leviticus 23:9–16; Deuteronomy 26:1–10; James 1:18

THE PASSOVER LAMB

The next day John saw Jesus coming toward him and said,
"Look, the Lamb of God, who takes away the sin of the world!"
John 1:29

Once a year, a Passover lamb was chosen and the table set. After a week of celebrating God's deliverance of His people from Egypt, the meal is eaten together, much like it was at the first Passover. The lamb is slaughtered and roasted, no bones in its body may be broken and none may be left until morning. In the first Passover meal, the lamb's blood was to be brushed over the doorframes so that the angel of death would pass over the homes of the Hebrews, while every home of the Egyptians lost the firstborn among them. It is this tragic showing of God's power, the last of the ten plagues, that moved Pharaoh to finally let the Egyptians go from their four hundred years of slavery. Ultimate delivery had come through God by the way of the blood of a lamb. Then, as God gave instructions for the work of the priests in His presence at the tabernacle or temple, He told them to offer one lamb every morning and every twilight (Exod. 29:38). This punctuated the days of God's people as a constant reminder of the spilling of blood required for atonement—for the purification and holiness of His people.

This is the context into which John proclaims Jesus as the Lamb of God: the One whose blood would be spilled so that the death angel would eternally pass over those covered by it. The blood of this Lamb would not simply protect us for the night, but forever. The Lamb has snatched us from the hands of the one who comes to steal, kill, and destroy, and delivered us into the Promised Land, a land flowing with milk and honey in which we will dwell with Him eternally.

It is during the week of Passover that Jesus shares the Last Supper with His disciples (Mark 14:12–16). The Lamb of God remembers the temporary deliverance of God out of Egypt, knowing that eternal deliverance was about to come through His death on the cross. It was later during this night that Jesus was arrested and tried. As He hung upon the cross days later, His bones were not broken, just like the bones of the Passover lamb and the prophecy found in Psalm 34:20, even when those around Him did receive that treatment (John 19:31–34). In the smallest detail, God was proclaiming Jesus as the Messiah He had promised all along.

Every year, God's people ate the Passover meal together celebrating the past deliverance out of Egypt but looking forward to when God would do it again through His promised Messiah. Although, they could not have imagined the glory of the deliverance Jesus would actually bring: He wouldn't be a military leader or a king like David, but He would come to deliver them from the worst of oppressors: sin and death. He would come to eternally reverse the curse.

Hebrews 9:11–14 says it this way, "But Christ has appeared as a high priest of the good things that have come. In the greater and more perfect tabernacle not made with hands (that is, not of this creation), he entered the most holy place once for all time, not by the blood of goats and calves, but by his own blood, having obtained eternal redemption. For if the blood of goats and bulls and the ashes of a young cow, sprinkling those who are defiled, sanctify for the purification of the flesh, how much more will the blood of Christ, who through the eternal Spirit offered himself without blemish to God, cleanse our consciences from dead works so that we can serve the living God?" We are not made whole and delivered through the blood of goats and calves, but by the blood of the Lamb of God who takes away the sins of the world. God sent His Son as a humble Lamb, headed to a sure slaughter. What love must this be that He would do this for our good? How unbelievable His commitment to His people, despite their rebellion, that He would deliver us so miraculously? And He is the "one like a slaughtered lamb standing in the midst of the throne" in Revelation 5:6, rightfully ruling as the One who laid down His life for His people.

"Look, the Lamb of God, who takes away the sin of the world" (John 1:29). Fix your eyes on Him today.

ADDITIONAL READING: Exodus 12:13; Isaiah 53:7; John 19:36; Revelation 12:11

THE LORD IS MY SHEPHERD, I SHALL NOT WANT

*"My sheep hear my voice, I know them, and they follow
me. I give them eternal life, and they will never perish.
No one will snatch them out of my hand. My Father,
who has given them to me, is greater than all. No one
is able to snatch them out of the Father's hand."*
John 10:27–29

F ew of you live on farms or have shepherded before. Shepherds in the
ancient Near East spent their days fighting off predators, cleaning and
shearing their sheep, anointing their heads with oil so pests would not terrorize
them, and caring for pastures so that they might eat. They also were required
to consistently watch the sheep because they unfailingly would wander off and
not know how to get home. Sheep are not the brightest bunch, often grazing
in a field until it was bare, consuming dirt and rocks if the shepherd did not
rotate them through pastures. They would also forget their need for water if
the shepherd did not lead them to a place where they could drink.

Imagine the thousands who were brought out of Egypt with Moses. I'm
sure their number dotted the hillside like the largest flock of Goshen. God

led them with a pillar of cloud by day and fire by night, shepherding them to greener pastures where they could experience His blessing: Canaan. He provided all they needed in the wilderness as they wandered: food, water, and clothes that never wore out, as well as His protective presence. God—Father, Son, and Spirit—have been shepherding His people since the beginning of time. He is a Good Shepherd.

> The Lord is my shepherd;
> I have what I need.
> He lets me lie down in green pastures;
> he leads me beside quiet waters.
> He renews my life;
> he leads me along the right paths
> for his name's sake.
> Even when I go through the darkest valley,
> I fear no danger,
> for you are with me;
> your rod and your staff—they comfort me.
> You prepare a table before me
> in the presence of my enemies;
> you anoint my head with oil;
> my cup overflows.
> Only goodness and faithful love will pursue me
> all the days of my life,
> and I will dwell in the house of the Lord
> as long as I live. (Ps. 23)

Shepherds are strong, brave, and consistent, working diligently to care for their sheep. When night comes and the sheep enter the pen, the shepherd sleeps across the threshold of the gate so that no predators can get in and harm the sheep while they are most vulnerable. Good shepherds are characterized by their provision and their kind care. Jesus claimed that He is the Shepherd of His people, and His sheep know His voice and follow Him. While sheep often wander off, our diligent Shepherd allows none to be snatched from the Father's hand. He provides the nourishment we need for spiritual wellness, providing Himself as the Bread of Life and the Living Water. Those who partake of these will never hunger or thirst again. He is the provision to end all provision; the portion that never depletes; the well that never runs dry. He is both the Provider and the Provision, and we are delivered into His care by the Father.

Perfect in all of His ways, Jesus guides and disciplines just as His sheep need. When we are injured, He binds our wounds, and when we are lost, He leaves the ninety-nine to find us. There is no need that He cannot meet or doesn't know. While the life of those in the flock is not a comfortable, safe life, there is peace and rest because the Shepherd is near, and He will and has laid down His life for His sheep.

> They will no longer hunger;
> they will no longer thirst;
> the sun will no longer strike them,
> nor will any scorching heat.
> For the Lamb who is at the center of the throne
> will shepherd them;
> he will guide them to springs of the waters of life,
> and God will wipe away every tear from their eyes.
> (Rev. 7:16–17)

ADDITIONAL READING: Micah 5:4; Hebrews 13:20–21; 1 Peter 5:4

HUNGRY NO MORE

"I am the bread of life," Jesus told them. "No one who comes to me will ever be hungry, and no one who believes in me will ever be thirsty again."
John 6:35

Flour, water, and salt—often yeast so the warm loaves rise, fluffy and soft. In the ancient Near East, baking bread was a liturgy of everyday life: reaping grain, milling it into flour, adding water and kneading and shaping it into loaves, baking it over an open flame. It was necessary to life, providing the needed energy for the day in a diet of bread, fruits and vegetables, and cheeses and oils. Meat was rarely consumed, and bread was the center of most meals. Yet, no matter how much of this bread was consumed, tomorrow would come and hungry bellies would rumble. In the wilderness, God gave His people manna to eat, literal "bread from heaven" (Exod. 16:4). It sustained their life in the most formative days as they learned to trust the God who led them. He allowed them to experience hunger as they wandered, but never let it go unanswered, as new manna was on the ground every morning, and a double portion on the day before the Sabbath so that they might have enough for both days. Yet still, hunger returned and the need for more persisted. God's intention for this provision was that His people "might learn that man does not live on bread alone but on every word that comes from the mouth of the LORD" (Deut. 8:3). While manna is certainly miraculous, there is a greater nourishment than any bread can offer, a greater provision than the provision of daily bread. While physical hunger returns to our belly, those who feast on Christ will never again be hungry because He truly satisfies.

Often in Scripture, we're invited to "taste and see that the LORD is good" (Ps. 34:8), to reverse the damage done by tasting and seeing that the fruit chosen in the first garden brings death and to eat of the One who has consumed the bitter cup of suffering in our place (Matt. 20:22). While festivals in the Old Testament proclaimed the coming Christ with full feasts, we now feast on Him as those who partake of His body as we await the fulfillment of this eating and drinking at the wedding supper of the Lamb. What we look forward to is also what the Israelites looked forward to, despite their not yet knowing it, as they celebrated in remembrance of God's great deliverance out of Egypt in their Passover meal. This meal was the one Jesus and His disciples partook at the Last Supper. There, Jesus gives the broken bread as a new physical reminder: His body, broken for our eternal rescue. Jesus "took bread, gave thanks, broke it, gave it to them, and said, "This is my body, which is given for you" (Luke 22:19).

This is the greater nourishment that we repeat as we receive communion together. We are part of what happened in Jesus's life, death, resurrection, and ascension, united in Him and communing with Him in the life of His church. While our bodies will get hungry, our soul finds rest and satisfaction because Jesus has paid our debt and made us right with God when we could do nothing to help ourselves. When we were utterly famished, dead in our lack of nourishment, He revived us through His body, broken for us. All who feast on Jesus, transformed by Him, will live forever.

Our spiritual hunger is fully and forever satisfied in Christ. The bread from heaven which fell in the wilderness provided for a day's hunger, but the Bread of Life provides for the hungers of an eternal life. The bread on the ground could only satisfy for a day, but the Bread of Life could satisfy forever. This is the Bread that we are asking for each day—not only the bread that fills our bellies but the bread that fills our hearts.

We are deeply dependent people, always finding something on which to rely for the strength we need for the day, but putting pressure on our relationships, our achievements, or even on ourselves will never provide the lasting rest that we need. We can find the strength to keep going by doing some self-care, giving ourselves a pep talk each morning, or developing the most strenuous schedule with habits to match. But these will always leave us wanting, and the more we rely on things that aren't God to fill the void created by the consequences of sin, the more they will eat away at us, leaving us malnourished and starving for more. Only the Bread of Life truly satisfies. He has provided for us through the breaking of His body. As we break bread that meets our momentary needs, may we praise God for meeting our greatest needs through the Son made flesh.

ADDITIONAL READING: Deuteronomy 8:1–10; Matthew 26:26–29; John 6:33, 51–53

56

NOTHING BUT THE TRUTH

"God is not a man, that he might lie,
or a son of man, that he might change his mind.
Does he speak and not act,
or promise and not fulfill?"
Numbers 23:19

The seed of the Enemy is doubt, but the seed of God is truth. When the first takes root in the soul, only death and destruction follow. It's like a weed, springing up quickly and, if left unchecked, it overwhelms the entirety of the crop, slowing or even preventing growth. When truth takes root, it's no longer weeds that flourish, but fruit.

Twisting the truth has been one of the Enemy's favorite strategies since the very beginning. He sowed doubt in the heart of Eve as he pushed, "Did God *really* say . . . ?" (Gen. 3:1, emphasis added). What if God didn't really mean what He said? What if He's not protecting us from the consequences of disobedience but is keeping us from something desirable? The Enemy may not deal in obvious, extreme lies. Instead, a tweak here and a twist there is far more successful at luring God's people into sin. When we aren't exactly sure or we struggle with doubting what God has said is true, we should take those concerns to Him rather than allowing the lie to take root in our soul. God is not so fragile that He cannot handle our questions. Eve didn't bring her doubt to Him so that He might root them out. Instead, she acted on that doubt, which sprang into disbelief, and began a chain reaction of the consequences of sin that will not cease until Jesus returns and banishes it for good. It's in that moment that doubt will be replaced not just with belief, but with sight. If only we lived with that end in mind.

Yet Balaam is correct in Numbers 23. Despite the King of Moab trying to hire Balaam to curse Israel, the Spirit spoke through him. A man whose integrity was lacking and even for sale proclaimed the perfect integrity of the Lord to His people. God is not a man that He should lie. He does not have a mind polluted by Adam and Eve's sin, but a holy, divine mind that is constant and unchanging. There is no word of God that He will leave unfulfilled. He has made known the way of life, and because He never lies, we can trust that His way is always best. He is completely unlike man in man's ability to speak falsity. God's voice builds worlds, and anything He says comes to being. He is not capable of lying or even accidentally misleading in any way. He never sows doubt or untruth. He only plants His Truth in the hearts of His people, so that it may grow and mature, bearing much fruit.

Truth is not just an affirmation of statements or doctrines. Truth is a Person. Truth finds its source and its definition in God, and there is no one who compares to His perfect, infinite truth. If He has said it, He will do it. If He has promised, it will be fulfilled. Today we trust all that God says and does because He is full of truth and never lies. But there comes a day when we won't take what God says on faith because we will see it with clear eyes and full hearts. We will see and understand fully.

The deception of a friend is crushing, but there is no deception in God. There is no contradiction in His truth. There's no exaggeration of the glories of heaven; no sugarcoating of judgment and wrath. There is no tweaking of the truth to be more palatable. He is only true, and there is no deception or unfaithfulness in Him at all. And if every word from the mouth of the Father, Son, and Spirit is true, then the wisest thing we can do is to listen.

God, give us ears to hear and eyes to see Your Truth. Give us discerning hearts and minds so that we may easily identify the whispers of the Enemy and see them for what they are: destruction and death. Help us love the Truth, both You who are Truth and the Words of Truth that You have given so we may live. In Jesus's name, amen.

ADDITIONAL READING: 1 Samuel 15:29; John 17:17; Hebrews 6:18

LASTING PEACE

Don't worry about anything, but in everything, through prayer
and petition with thanksgiving, present your requests to God.
And the peace of God, which surpasses all understanding,
will guard your hearts and minds in Christ Jesus.
Philippians 4:6–7

Every day, you and I process 100,000 words or 34 gigabytes of information (on average) in our leisure time.[38] That's the equivalent of some 174 newspapers a day, five times as much as we consumed each day in 1986,[39] and not while we sit at our desks, but while we "rest and recharge." And this was the data for 2011, just imagine what it is today before many of the current social media platforms existed. We have access to the world's heartache at our fingertips, not just experiencing media overload but compassion fatigue, a term once reserved for only those serving the most vulnerable in tragic circumstances.[40] Needing to care about all the things we need to care about in the world has us burned out and inconsolably anxious. We are built for life in tiny villages where support and care are built in and your neighbor's sadness doesn't have to be compared to the unbelievable tragedy on the other side of the world because those aren't even known. Yet we are living in the information age where the more shocking, brutal, and heart-breaking, the better. The economy of attention is built on clicks, and the strategy is working. Families, coworkers, and strangers in a waiting room together are more likely to sit with their nose in their device than they are to engage with one another, and it's making us isolated, overwhelmed, and completely without peace.

So what's the way out of our frenzied minds and frenzied feeds? "Don't worry about anything, but in everything, through prayer and petition with thanksgiving, present your requests to God" (Phil. 4:6). Why? Because He's the God of Peace, the One who orders chaos (1 Cor. 14:33). In communing with Him, peace is automatic.

God has given us a place to take the fear and worry we face. He has invited us into His throne room, allowing us to drop our heavy bags and leave them for a lighter life of abundance with Christ. Yet, it's as if these heavy bags are tied to our arms and we are helpless to cut the ropes ourselves. God does miraculous work in us through His ministry of prayer, and it is when we bring Him what weighs us down that He may remove it, giving us His peace that surpasses all understanding.

Christ has brought eternal peace with God for His people through His death on the cross, paying the penalty of sin, and raising victorious over it, and He has ascended, advocating for this peace before the Father. We have found safety in Christ as our eternal hiding place. We need not worry or fear because He holds authority over all. There is nothing that can snatch us from His hand and the eternal peace that awaits us. He is the Prince of Peace (Isa. 9:6), and not just some day in the future. But He is our Prince of Peace today, quieting our souls and bearing our heavy yokes so we don't have to.

Paul often calls us to pursue peace in his letters, and not just peace with God, but also peace with others. When we are hidden in Christ, operating rightly as His body in His church which is the outpost of the kingdom of heaven on earth, our unity in His body is the bond of our peace (Eph. 4:2–3). Peace with God and peace with others brings the internal peace we so desperately desire. And it's Jesus who has secured it for us through His resurrection that proves victory over all we fear. God is peace, and He can be nothing that He is not. And through Christ, He cultivates this peace for us.

In 1739, Charles Wesley wrote what later became the hymn "O for a Thousand Tongues to Sing." The second stanza reads: "Jesus! The Name that charms our fears, that bids our sorrows cease; 'Tis music in the sinner's ears, 'Tis life and health and peace."[41] Jesus has become the conduit of God's peace to us. May we spend today dropping our heavy weights and enjoying the peace that surpasses understanding.

ADDITIONAL READING: Psalm 4:8; Isaiah 26:3; Matthew 11:28; Colossians 3:15

58

THE WEIGHT OF HIS GLORY

The cloud covered the tent of meeting, and the glory
of the LORD filled the tabernacle. Moses was unable to
enter the tent of meeting because the cloud rested on it,
and the glory of the LORD filled the tabernacle.
Exodus 40:34–35

G lory. Beauty. Majesty. Awe.

The glory of the Lord is overwhelming, so much so, that when it filled the tabernacle in Exodus 40, even Moses, who had stood in the Lord's presence multiple times, could not enter. Isaiah saw a tiny glimpse of the immensity of God in His vision in Isaiah 6:1, when just the hem of His robe filled the temple. Around His throne are the seraphim, the "burning ones," with six wings that are proclaiming the holiness of God, the temple filled with smoke and the thresholds shook at their voice (v. 4). The Holy of Holies, where God's presence dwelled in the tabernacle and temple could only be entered once a year by the high priest on the Day of Atonement with much fear and trembling (Lev. 16). As His glory moved toward the temple to fill it in Ezekiel, "His voice sounded like the roar of a huge torrent, and the earth shone with his glory" (Ezek. 43:2). This glory is the expression of the fullness of His infinite attributes, the experience of His beauty, not in aesthetics, although His beauty is beyond imagination, but in the beauty of His Person, the immensity and overwhelming otherness of the Godhead. In Exodus 33, Moses asks to see this fullness, and God obliges, hiding in the cleft of the rock and allowing him to see just His back because to see His face would be too much. His glory was too wonderful—too weighty—for Moses to view it in totality. His flesh could not bear it. His mind could not comprehend.

The weight of His totality should bring us to our knees. It's unfathomably good. And yet, what Moses, Isaiah, Ezekiel, the priests, and others throughout Scripture saw in part we see in full in Christ. He is "the radiance of God's glory and the exact expression of his nature" (Heb. 1:3). The fullness of the beauty of His attributes are found in the humble King born in a manger. This is a glory unlike any the ancient world had seen. He did not wear a victor's crown or command armies, but He was and is forever glorious: one with the Father and Spirit, magnificent in all His ways. It is through His humility that He would become man and dwell among us, taking on all the maladies of the flesh while also being fully God. It is this humility that made a way for us to experience God's glory, too. We see it in Christ and we experience it through the indwelling of the Spirit. The glory that once kept God's people out of the holiest place because of God's great holiness and their impurity now invites us in through the holiness applied to us through Jesus. This is the glory that brings us to our knees and raises us to shout with joy—that we see God when we fix our eyes on Jesus. We see the fullness of God's glory in the Son made flesh.

To look upon Jesus is to see the glory of God. He has invited us to experience it fully by trusting Jesus, participating in the divine life through Him. The experienced presence of God, the fullness of His holiness, the goodness of all that He is has been given to you in Christ. This is the presence that moved people immediately to worship, fear, and trembling throughout millennia. We would do well to do a bit more fear and trembling of the glorious, magnificent God that we serve. He is not just "the man upstairs" or "our BFF." He is glorious and holy, to be approached in righteousness. The glory of the Christian life is that we do get to approach Him in righteousness because, when God looks at us, He sees the righteousness of Jesus.

How are you sitting in amazement at the glory of God today? How are you making sure that you stay overwhelmed by the beauty of the One you serve? He is glorious! May it both bring us to our knees in prayer and raise us to our feet in worship. What an overwhelmingly good God we serve, and He has willingly given His goodness to us in the experience of His glory. How are you responding to the weightiness of His glory in your life? Are you seeking it or is it easier to avoid such weight?

ADDITIONAL READING: Exodus 15:11; Exodus 33:18–23; 1 Chronicles 29:11; Ezekiel 10:4; Habakkuk 2:14; John 17:5

59

SOVEREIGN

I form light and create darkness,
I make success and create disaster;
I am the LORD, who does all these things.
"Heavens, sprinkle from above,
and let the skies shower righteousness.
Let the earth open up
so that salvation will sprout
and righteousness will spring up with it.
I, the LORD, have created it.
"Woe to the one who argues with his Maker—
one clay pot among many.
Does clay say to the one forming it,
'What are you making?'
Or does your work say,
'He has no hands'?"
Isaiah 45:7–9

W̲e serve a God who compels Pharoah to let His people go (even hard-
ening his heart after he had often hardened it himself) and who

raises up nations to execute judgment on His people. He has both absolute authority and control over the happenings of the world, yet He does not exercise this authority and control with an iron fist of determination, as if He is the acting agent in every decision and step we take. Instead, God has given us the freedom to live and move as we desire, making clear that His way is always the best because all things, no matter which choice you make, are moving toward His cosmic end. While some scholars disagree on the details of God's control—whether it's dynamic with some reliance on human action (Arminian position), or an outworking of God's foreknowledge (Molinist position), or if every detail is already part of His eternal plan (Reformed position), they all agree God is exercising His divine sovereignty in His world.

I'm partial to Gregg Allison's definition of God's providential sovereignty, which he defines as "the continuing work of God to preserve, cooperate in ongoing activities of the created order, and govern His creation."[42] God did not wind up His creation like a music box and walk away. His sovereignty proclaims that He is actively engaged in the world at large and the tiniest details of your life. This passage in Isaiah 45:7–9 reads similarly to Job, which is often the go-to illustration of God's sovereignty over all because the authority of God to move in ways we do not understand is so clear in his story. While we don't always understand why exactly things happen in His sovereignty, like Job, we can still trust that He is good and He is working, both around us and in us.

Isaiah proves the incomprehensibility of God's work in the passage above, highlighting God's sovereign understanding and our incredibly limited vision. It's nonsense that a clay pot would speak to its Potter, directing His hands, but that is precisely what we seek to do. Other translations handle the final question of the pot here as "'Your work has no handles'?" (ESV). What we might view as integral to the vessel, the Lord sovereignly leaves out. Why? We don't know, but we know it is good, right, and just, and we know it is as God intended because, while He holds no bounds, all things are within the bounds of His sovereignty. Nothing is outside of His design.

Does this mean that we might find ourselves wishing we had a handle? That life was different and that God had exercised His sovereign control in a way that seemed more good and right to our finite minds? Yes. I've felt that and I'm sure you have too. We aren't always given the gift of being able to connect the dots between what happens in our life and what God is doing for His broader purposes. It's in those moments that we can only rest in what we know to be true of the nature of God, that He is always our highest good, even if our idea of good is lacking. Because He is infinite in His knowledge and kindness, it is always our view that is jaded or dimmed in right understanding, not His character. His ways are always intended for His greatest glory. Only the Potter knows the intended use for the design while it's on His wheel and shaped under the force of His hand. He can be trusted as He designs you for His purposes, even if you think you look silly without a handle.

ADDITIONAL READING: Job 42:2; Lamentations 3:37–39; Romans 8:28; Colossians 1:16–17

KIND, NOT NICE

But when the goodness and loving kindness of God our Savior
appeared, he saved us, not because of works done by us in
righteousness, but according to his own mercy, by the washing of
regeneration and renewal of the Holy Spirit, whom he poured out on
us richly through Jesus Christ our Savior, so that being justified by
his grace we might become heirs according to the hope of eternal life.
Titus 3:4–7 ESV

I've always told my kids I'd rather them be kind than anything else in the world. Smart, athletic, a leader . . . all great. But more than these, my hope for them is that they'll grow up to be kind. Kind, not necessarily nice.

Kindness is not synonymous with niceness—the sugary sweet politeness that often conceals the truth behind a fake smile if it is the tiniest bit uncomfortable. True kindness considers what is best for the other, pursuing both a relationship or a holding of presence with one another, and opportunities to serve through word and deed. Kindness may mean delivering hard truths, but always with much love and a desire for reconciliation and righteousness. It may also mean sacrificing something you hold dear (time, money, resources) for the betterment of another. Kindness protects and serves the other, while niceness protects and serves self.

God is not one to serve us niceties, telling us what we want to hear and avoiding conflict at all costs. Instead, He is both a God of love and of justice, of gentleness and discipline. These are held in tension in His kindness, but tension doesn't truly describe the inner workings of God in His attributes. His nature isn't made up of a list of individual attributes that act apart from one another and might be at war with one another at times. This is how the inner lives of humanity works, where flesh and spirit wrestle just as love and disdain do. Our God is not like this because He is One and His attributes cannot be separated from one another nor from Him. God doesn't just act kind. He is kindness, and His ultimate kindness is seen in Christ.

Jesus has laid down His life for His friends, and what a glory that He would call us friends, wayward as we are. He bore the righteous requirement of God's justice for our sin and discipline for rebellion in His body in His agony on the cross. He is the prize of salvation, the kind gift of God. God has poured out His presence on us in the incarnation of the Son and in the indwelling of the Spirit. The gospel is God's kindness to us—that God has done for us what we desperately needed to take us from death to life—but a gift we wouldn't have even known to ask for. His kindness is in His discipline, as He convicts us through the Spirit to be conformed to the image of Christ, again, giving us what doesn't always feel nice but is always kind. He has justified us by grace, making us heirs with hope of eternal life through His kindness, an always loving, always for-the-betterment-of-others-even-when-it-means-stepping-on-their-toes kind of love. God is both breaking us down and remaking us, calling us to uncomfortable repentance and overwhelming us with grace when we do.

Often, we want God to just be nice—answer our prayers precisely how we'd like them to be answered; provide in the ways that we believe we should receive provision; and encourage us with all the things we are doing well, leaving out anything that falls short. But then, God would be nice, but He wouldn't be kind. It wouldn't be kind to let us call the shots, because we make really terrible gods for ourselves. We are not omniscient, despite our desire to be. We don't know what is truly best for us or for the cosmic plan God is working throughout all of history that furthers His kingdom and culminates in His eternal renewal and reign. He is not nice, but He is kind.

How have you hoped God would be nice to you in the past? In what ways has He been kind?

ADDITIONAL READING: Psalm 63:3; Psalm 145:8–13; Isaiah 63:7

SELF-SUFFICIENT, SELF-EXISTENT, AND SELF-GIVING

Neither is he served by human hands, as though he needed anything, since he himself gives everyone life and breath and all things. From one man he has made every nationality to live over the whole earth and has determined their appointed times and the boundaries of where they live.
Acts 17:25–26

From the moment of conception, our life is wholly dependent upon another. Another provides all we need for life: food, water, oxygen, a womb that regulates our temperature. And this is the unconscious kindness of a mother. A new kind of dependence is birthed with each baby. Every moment of safety and provision is reliant upon the hands of a caregiver. Into adulthood, we project an ability to care for ourselves—to be self-sufficient, but it is only an illusion. Even if you grow all of your food in your garden, spin your own thread to sew your own clothes, and learn architecture to build your own home, you continue your dependence on God who gives and sustains life. You may feed, clothe, or house yourself, but you cannot be the source of life itself.

We are innately needy, reliant upon God to give us life and to sustain the earth so that we may also join Him in the work of providing for those needs. We are innately needy, but God is innately self-sufficient. He exists of and from Himself, never relying on any other. He has no needs. There is nothing we could offer Him that He doesn't already have, and there is nothing we could tell Him that He doesn't already know. He has no need of provision, information, or communion. He is perfectly whole, divinely independent, holding all divine freedom. He has perfect communion within Himself as Father, Son, and Spirit.

He did not create because He was lonely, as if we could offer Him the companionship that He desired. He has not allowed us to participate in His kingdom-building because He couldn't do it without us. He has created us and engaged with us out of love, not out of need. He sets our boundaries because He is boundary-less. He determines our times because He is time-less. He sustains because He is without need for sustaining. He gives us life because He *is* life itself. It is here that we find the greatest Creator/creature distinction. He is so unlike us, and yet so involved with our every moment. He is above all, unlimited in His capacity or abilities. This aseity, or independence, is often viewed as the first of His attributes,[43] the one through which the others flow. He can enter into creation's needs as the Provider because He is not a Provider who needs a source. He can make and keep covenants because He is not reliant on anything but Himself for fulfilling it. Nothing can thwart His plan or interrupt His intention. He is unchanging and unbound by time, an experience so different than our own, as every moment has a time stamp and progress is always forward motion.

Yet, in Christ, He became needy for us. He took on flesh in all its ailments and boundaries, drinking the cup of human suffering to the dregs, while also feeling the anguish of desiring another way to reconcile us to

God, as drops of blood fell from His head as He prayed in the garden of Gethsemane. The One who has no need became needy for us so we'd never have an unmet spiritual need again. Through His life, death, resurrection, and ascension, we share in His riches, independent of any giver but Him. It is because of His full independence and freedom that we have independence from the grips of evil and freedom from the chains of sin. We experience these kindnesses only in Christ—He is their location.

What are your needs today? How do you need to trust the One who has no needs, but who holds authority over all things, able to meet your need without fail because of His aseity, or His total independence. Praise God—He is unbound and unhindered, and in all of His independence, He is moving and working, not for a selfish benefit but for His praise and the eternal good of His people.

ADDITIONAL READING: Exodus 3:13–15; Psalm 24:1; John 5:26; Romans 11:36

EVERY NEED SUPPLIED

And my God will supply all your needs according
to his riches in glory in Christ Jesus.
Philippians 4:19

A woman facing the sorrow of losing her husband now faced the impossible: she owed a debt she could not pay, having only a single jar of oil in her home. She had two sons, and feared they would be made slaves as payment for this debt. She came lamenting to Elisha, asking for help. He encouraged her to collect empty jars from her neighbors, and not just one or two. He said, "Do not get just a few" (2 Kings 4:3).

She collected jars and went into her home and did just as Elisha instructed, pouring oil into all the containers. As she did, one after another filled. Her sons brought her more jars, until there were no more to be found, each one filling with oil until the last one. The woman—astonished, I'm sure—returned to Elisha and told him what had happened. He told her, "Go sell the oil and pay your debt; you and your sons can live on the rest" (v. 7).

Pay your debt and live on the rest. God not only provided what she needed that day to guard against the enslavement of her sons because of the debt. This provision was lavish and surprising, meeting an impossible moment with a miraculous end that gave them what they needed not only that day, but beyond.

Now, God is also working to meet greater needs than our physical needs, and this is what Paul writes about in Philippians 4. There may be physical needs that are left unmet on this side of heaven because sin has entered the world and infected every atom. Every system is broken under its weight. There is no formula we can engage to force God to bless us generously with any sort of prosperity or health. While He can and does intervene in situations like this widow's, He doesn't every time; but this does not detract from His generosity.

There are still people who go to bed hungry or without shelter, who face the dangers of war and persecution. There are people who lose jobs and struggle to pay bills and people who walk difficult roads full of medical appointments and scary diagnoses. Suffering is sure—part of our experience as humans—but Philippians 4 refers to a greater need: the need for a thriving spiritual life with Christ, full of the riches of His glory to be experienced by those who love Him. Paul wrote this in prison, and we can assume his physical needs abounded. But His spiritual life was flourishing. For those in Christ, suffering can be joy because contentment is not based on what you have, but Who you have. He has been generous to us with His presence, sustaining and comforting us. The Father and Son have sent the Spirit, closer than the heart beating in our chest, so that in our need, we may never be alone.

The Father did not *have* to send the Son so we might know Him and be made right with Him. The Father and Son did not *have* to send the Spirit so we would have God Himself indwelling us, making us bold and applying to our hearts the generous gifts available to us through Jesus. The Father, Son, and Spirit did not *have* to get involved in the messiness of our lives, meeting our needs or hearing our cries. *But He did.* And He does. Infinitely so.

How has the Lord been generous to you? Spend some time thanking Him for His generosity today.

ADDITIONAL READING: Psalm 36:7–8; Matthew 7:7–11; Romans 8:32; James 1:17

NO BOUNDS; NO LIMITS

He is the blessed and only Sovereign, the King of kings,
and the Lord of lords, who alone is immortal and who
lives in unapproachable light, whom no one has seen or
can see, to him be honor and eternal power. Amen.
1 Timothy 6:15b–16

We live in a world of limitations. Limitations of time like beginnings and endings, starts and stops. Births and deaths. Limitations of capacity like intelligence and wisdom, unable to pull multiple all-nighters or hold heavy weights for an extended period. Limitations of space and distance, like being double-booked and desiring home, but being on the other side of the world.

Often, when we consider God's infinitude, we only think about His existence being without beginning or end, stretching as far as the east is from the west in an unending horizon line of ages and eras. This is a testimony to His infinitude, but it is not the fullness of it. His infinitude is not held to a single category because God is One, so everything that is true of God is infinite. His love, His justice, His kindness, His sovereignty, His power, His goodness—all are without bounds and are completely limitless.

He has no beginning or end but is so infinitely beyond these categories that He actually *is* the beginning and end (Rev. 1:8), containing them in Himself, their source and author.

Infinitude communicates the never-stopping, never-lessened, never-dimmed-in-any-way-from-its-total-perfection nature of God. Every one of His attributes is from eternity to eternity, which is not a unit of measure we can chart. This is not a truth we will fully grasp on this side of heaven, but it is worthy of our contemplation, because the more our minds find that they cannot begin to express the magnitude of God, the more we love Him. He bestows gifts and shares attributes with humanity without depleting any resource, able to give fully to all of His children because He has no limits.

This is a truth presented across the whole of Scripture. He is the One before the beginning in Genesis 1 and John 1, and we see His boundless attributes experienced in the history of God's people and in the praise that guides their days. It's His infinite presence that allows Him to be in all places at all times, hearing and answering every prayer, despite the millions raising their voice simultaneously. His attention is never divided because He is infinite. His ways are always good because this infinitude extends to His knowledge, power, and goodness. He is unlimited in the way He may solve problems, even when we see only one solution. He is no mere mortal; He is the sovereign King of kings and Lord of lords. He is infinite in honor and power. He is the blessed One Timothy proclaims in the verse above.

There is no obstacle that thwarts Him and He bows to no other authority. How would we live differently if this truth really sunk into our hearts? How would we pray differently? Serve differently?

No matter the frustration we find as we press against our own limits, we serve a God who is infinitely infinite. Whatever you face today, He can do far beyond what you imagine and cultivate good out of what seems to be hopeless. His ways are higher and better, even when we can't make sense of them. He is infinitely good, even when our situation is not. There is none like our God, and He calls you child.

Have you found yourself at the end of your limits? How might you find hope and joy in His infinitude today? Spend some time contemplating God's attributes and the implications of His limitlessness in each one. Record some of these truths so that you can revisit them on the days you forget. Store up hope for a day when you need it. He is boundless in His goodness, even His goodness to you.

ADDITIONAL READING: 1 Kings 8:27; Psalm 147:5; Isaiah 40:28; Revelation 19:6

64

THE SECOND GREATEST GIFT

*Peter replied, "Repent and be baptized, each of you, in
the name of Jesus Christ for the forgiveness of your sins,
and you will receive the gift of the Holy Spirit. For the
promise is for you and for your children, and for all who
are far off, as many as the Lord our God will call."*
Acts 2:38–39

Every few years, The State of Theology report is released by Lifeway
Research and Ligonier Ministries. I'm showing you a little too clearly
how much of a nerd I am here, but I love this research, and I wait for it
like a child waits for Christmas. While it isn't the happiest of news, it gives
us a clear vision of what people who self-identify as Christians in America
believe about God. In 2022, this research found that 59 percent of respondents believe that the Holy Spirit is a force, rather than a personal being,
with another 15 percent who were unsure. That leaves only 26 percent of
respondents affirming Him as a Person.[44] Yet, this gift—the Spirit—is not
some nameless otherworldly force, as though He could be equated with the
force of gravity. He is a Person, united with the Father and Son and indwelling His people.

While He is the Third Person of the Trinity, He is not third in a hierarchy. God is not divided, as if there could be some sort of ordering of His Persons within His Oneness. Third is also not an indication of chronology, because there has never been a time when the Three Persons were not or a time when they were not One. Third simply indicates the Father as source, the Son as begotten, and the Spirit as proceeding from Father and Son. Each person is coequal, coeternal, and consubstantial. They are distinct, but also are perfectly united in one another. He, too, is God, and He is the gift of God to His people. This is our second greatest gift, only second to the gift of salvation through Jesus securing it, making the gift of the Holy Spirit possible. This gift is to participate in the life of the Godhead, indwelled by the Spirit, united in Christ, and drawn close to the Father through the ministry of the Son and the Spirit.

In the passage above, the Spirit had just fallen at Pentecost, and the fruit He was creating in the people of God was astounding. The church was growing by the thousands day after day, and the gospel was going forth to the nations. The Spirit was bringing life to old bones, resurrecting them from death to life in Christ. He is the life-giving power that raised Jesus from the dead, and the life-giving power that opened your eyes to your need for the Savior. He is the gift we receive immediately upon trusting Christ, a sort of home-warming homecoming gift, sent by the Father and Son to secure us until the day Jesus returns and we see God face-to-face in all His glory. The Spirit is the greatest gift we receive outside of our salvation—Jesus Himself. He is the presence of God in our life, moving and active both in our lives and all around us today, speaking what the Father and Son say and reminding us of Jesus's teaching; guiding us in righteousness; and filling us with the peace, joy, and comfort that only God can give. Through Him, we become partakers of grace and participants of the divine life. Second Peter 1:2–4 says it this way: "May grace and peace be multiplied to you through the knowledge of God and of Jesus our Lord. His divine power has given us everything required for life and godliness through the knowledge of him who called us by his own glory and goodness. By these he has given us very great and precious promises, so that through them you may share in the divine nature, escaping the corruption that is in the world because of evil desire."

May we participate well. May we receive well. May we operate under the guidance of the Spirit, allowing Him to prune our lives of what does not please God so that we may draw into deeper fellowship with God. What an immeasurable gift! He hasn't only dwelled *with* us, He has dwelled *in* us. Celebrate this good gift today.

ADDITIONAL READING: Nehemiah 9:20; Luke 11:13; John 14:26; Acts 2:38–39; Acts 5:32; 1 Peter 4:14

GOD OF ALL COMFORT

*Blessed be the God and Father of our Lord Jesus Christ, the
Father of mercies and the God of all comfort. He comforts us
in all our affliction, so that we may be able to comfort those
who are in any kind of affliction, through the comfort we
ourselves receive from God. For just as the sufferings of Christ
overflow to us, so also through Christ our comfort overflows.*
2 Corinthians 1:3–5

The details of everyday life are easily forgotten, just chalk on the side-walk, waiting to be swept away by the rain. The details of grief, on the other hand, are more like splashes of paint. At twelve, I was awakened in the middle of the night by my mom whose face was tear-stained and my pastor, who had come to be with us, an embodied sense of God's comforting presence. My dad, who had suffered through cancer for four years, had gone to be with the Lord. I still remember that moment like it was yesterday. I can tell you what my brother's shoes looked like, because they laid in my line of sight as I stared at the floor. Sometimes I see them in my mind, taking me back more than twenty years in an instant. The nature of grief is circular, boomerang-like in its return to the tender stages long after you feel it is appropriate to find yourself there again.

As I've grown, I've found there to be more opportunities for grief. Recently, I found myself asking a friend if everyone around us was falling apart or if I'm just finally adult enough to truly know about the deep suffering of others. In these seasons of suffering, whether the trials are wounds I'll carry forever or those I try to shoulder alongside my hurting brothers and sisters, I've found the Spirit to comfort in ways that surpass my comprehension.

Logic does not lead us to peace. Believe me, I've tried. I've coached my brain to think through all the possible reasons for events, which led me to be more informed, but also more anxious and grieved than before. Even if we had access to the answers we so desperately seek from the Lord—the why? Why me? Why them? Why now? Why this?—our hearts would still not find rest. Reason does not develop peace. The brokenness of the world and the steps of God cannot be parsed or plumbed with human faculties. Yet there is comfort deeper still.

The Spirit, with deeper groanings than we can hear, intercedes on our behalf (Rom. 8:26), and in our weakest, the Spirit draws ever nearer. It's not that He's been away when suffering hasn't been at the forefront of our lives, but suffering slices open our hearts, exposing what had long been hidden away anew. The raw flesh exposed to the rushing wind of His Spirit keeps your attention because it is raw. Have you ever cut your finger with a sharp knife in the kitchen? The ceiling fan you ignored suddenly becomes your mind's fixation as the moving air brings a new tenderness to the wound. The movement of our God of comfort alerts us to His presence, where joy and rest reside.

Whatever the grief that boomerangs in your life, I pray that these moments of tenderness awaken your heart to His movement, to His comfort. He may not remove grief, suffering, or injustice on this side of heaven, but He promises to walk it with us, one day at a time. Isaiah 61 looks forward to this day. Meditate on it as we remember the God who is Comfort today:

> The Spirit of the Lord GOD is on me,
> because the LORD has anointed me
> to bring good news to the poor.
> He has sent me to heal the brokenhearted,
> to proclaim liberty to the captives
> and freedom to the prisoners;
> to proclaim the year of the LORD's favor,
> and the day of our God's vengeance;
> to comfort all who mourn,
> to provide for those who mourn in Zion;
> to give them a crown of beauty instead of ashes,
> festive oil instead of mourning,
> and splendid clothes instead of despair.
> And they will be called righteous trees,
> planted by the LORD
> to glorify him.
> (Isa. 61:1–3)

ADDITIONAL READING: Psalm 34:18; Isaiah 51:12; John 14:27

GIFTS FOR THE COMMON GOOD

Now there are different gifts, but the same Spirit. There are different
ministries, but the same Lord. And there are different activities,
but the same God works all of them in each person. A manifestation
of the Spirit is given to each person for the common good.
1 Corinthians 12:4–7

During my college years, I ran cross-country. (Not because I was fast; I most certainly was not. To compete at races as a team, they needed five girls and they only had four. Many on the team were friends of mine, so they lured me in with promises of prerace carb loading and lots of extra hanging out during practices.) As we ran our warm-up miles each day, we'd often chat about the other sports teams we could see practicing as we ran. "Baseball— how boring. All they do is stand around waiting on a ball." "Soccer. They just run back and forth on a tiny field for hours. How confining." As early twenty-somethings, we lacked the self-awareness to realize our sport was literally just putting one foot in front of the other as quickly as possible.

What is true about each of the teams we passed, and even the one we were on, was the required coordination every athlete needed both individually and corporately. We needed to perform at our best, not tripping over our own feet or going out too fast from the starting line and tiring long before the finish. We needed to work together as a pack as much as possible, staying tight, but also cheering each other on because all five of our times counted, and it was the team time—the composite—that determined how we ranked. Of course, with baseball or soccer, you need even more coordination for great plays and defense, runs and goals. On a team, every member has a part to play, every member has gifts meant for use.

God has given you gifts for use in His kingdom to edify His church. The breadth of gifts is as varied as the joints, hands, marrow, and organs of the body. These parts make up the whole of the body of Christ, the church who is to be the vision of heaven on earth. Each gift is prepared for God's kingdom purposes by the Father, directed by Christ for use in the church, and given by the Spirit when He seals us for salvation. The gift is not for the gifted, but to be used in and for the church; not for our own glory or applause, but for His. And the body, the church, needs your gift. Do you think you might be a liver when you'd rather be a mouth, teaching about Him? Or you wonder if you might be a spleen when you'd rather be feet, going to faraway lands to take the gospel? There is no one who is in Christ—part of His body—who is not necessary to the flourishing of the church. The body will suffer without that liver to dispose of what is poisonous or spleen to fight off incoming (germ) attacks.

Like my team of five runners, we need you. Everyone has to participate. As Jesus is a gift to us, we are to be a gift to one another. As we are united to Him, we are united to one another in His body. God is both saving each of His children and His church as a whole. He is both sanctifying each part and His body as a whole. You have been saved to a community of faith, not a life of solitary pursuit. And that community of faith is equipped to serve by God Himself. The One who knows every need is meeting them through the church. You are a gift—your presence, your care, the particular way God has wired you to serve His kingdom. Your gifts are for the building up of the only eternal structure, the church, and the lives of eternal people, for the work of preparation. This place is not our home. We are preparing one another for life in another kingdom, exercising our gifts to edify the church so that we all might long for heaven all the more as we get small glimpses of it.

What spiritual gifts has the Spirit given to you? As Basil of Caesarea rightly said: "There is not one single gift which reaches creation without the Holy Spirit."[45]

Read 1 Corinthians 12 and Ephesians 4:11–13 to explore some of the gifts of the Spirit. Even if you feel God has given you a spot on the "boring" baseball team, know that the body of Christ needs your gift. You are a gift, and the Holy Spirit desires that you use your gifts for the glory of God through His power. We need you, and we thank God for your giftedness.

How is He cultivating one of these in you? How are you serving Him with it?

ADDITIONAL READING: Romans 12:1–8; 1 Corinthians 12:12–31; 1 Peter 4:10–11

A GUIDE INTO ALL TRUTH

"When the Spirit of truth comes, he will guide you into all
the truth. For he will not speak on his own, but he will speak
whatever he hears. He will also declare to you what is to come."
John 16:13

A week's worth of decisions is enough to crush even the most enthu-
siastic planner. No amount of hours in the day can afford the time
necessary to extrapolate every decision's potential effects across the following
years or even decades of your life. And even if we could, would we want to?

In my early years in adult life, I was so afraid that I might choose
the wrong husband or the wrong career. That somehow, despite my best
attempts, I would thwart the will of God and royally destroy His plan for
my life. Today, I know that I don't hold that kind of power, and neither
do you.

God has not heaped pressure on us to tirelessly search out His hidden
will that He has buried deep below the surface of His Word. We do not toil
as those looking for a needle in a haystack, distracted every few moments
by the hay-fever-induced sneezing. God's will is not buried treasure, and it's
no needle in a haystack. Not only has God given us His Word, where He

clearly displays His intentions and how one might live under the glory of His way that leads to life, He has also given us His Spirit. Though our eyes may fail us in the reading of God's Word and our feet may fail to carry us to His church where we may hear it taught, the Spirit within His people never fails to remind us of His truth. While God has never written my necessary next step in the sky or spoken audibly about where I should live, what I should do for work, or who I should build relationships with, He consistently moves me to look more and more like Jesus, to be more involved in His church, and to love His Word. God is concerned with who we are becoming and gives us the freedom to seek Him in whatever set of circumstances and in whatever opportune decisions we find ourselves. Christian, He is far more committed to your holiness than to whatever decisions are keeping you up at night. Seek to follow Him. Spend time with Him. And allow the Spirit, as your guide, to do the rest.

The Spirit only speaks what the Father and Son declare. The triune God indwells you, and as He promised Israel, "and whenever you turn to the right or to the left, your ears will hear this command behind you: 'This is the way. Walk in it'" (Isa. 30:21). This promise is wedged between God's pronouncement of coming judgment for those who have oppressed God's people. A day would come when the Egyptians would not tell them where to walk or where to make bricks. A day would come when the Assyrians would no longer have the power to demand their feet to walk to a foreign land, exiled from the land God gave and His glorious blessings that overflowed there. There would come a day when a brutal empire would not prevail because the Spirit would break the chains of enslavement and bring forth the joy of being led by the omnipotent, always good God who can do no wrong and certainly can do no wrong to you. He's the One who will guide you. His guidance is always toward the ways of Christ.

This is the test of that guidance: Does this lead me closer to the freedom of Christ or the enslavement of the brutal dictator who comes to kill and steal and destroy? Despite the Enemy's cunning deception that causes us to often believe that the evil of sin is good and actually leads to life or true freedom, the Spirit is the better guide. He is the One who speaks to us; the One who gives freedom, who opens our eyes to our sin so that He may root it out and who leads us into deeper love for Christ, deeper hunger for His Word, and deeper thirst for His ways. You have a guide. No decision is your own to figure out the way forward. The pressure is off. You have a God who is near.

How do you need Him to guide you today? Where have you listened to the instructions of the Enemy as to what to do or where to go? Spend some time asking Him to guide you with power so that you might look more and more like the Savior you serve.

ADDITIONAL READING: Proverbs 3:5–6; Proverbs 16:9; Matthew 7:7–11; James 1:5

ILLUMINATING OUR EYES

*"Nevertheless, I am telling you the truth. It is for your benefit that
I go away, because if I don't go away the Counselor will not come
to you. If I go, I will send him to you. When he comes, he will
convict the world about sin, righteousness, and judgment: About
sin, because they do not believe in me; about righteousness, because
I am going to the Father and you will no longer see me; and about
judgment, because the ruler of this world has been judged."*
John 16:7–11

Isn't it strange that we can walk in the darkest of spaces, and still perceive light? The longer you spend in a dark room, the clearer your vision seems to become as the rods and cones in your eyes adapt and your pupils widen to let in any trace of it. Light invades what seems to be utter darkness. A single candle in the labyrinth of a cave illuminates each step, even miles under the ground.

There's no shortage of fumbling moments in the darkness in our lives. Even after we meet the One who is truly wise, we run toward the darkness that somehow entices us to believe it's safer there, better, or more fun. Yet there is One who meets us in that darkness. He opens our eyes so that we may truly see what the eyes of our body cannot, but the eyes of hearts widen in the joy of what is seen—of Who is seen.

Jesus said that it was better for Him to go than to stay with His disciples, a shocking truth for those who were standing face-to-face with the Savior of the world. How, Lord? The Spirit He would send would open the eyes of their hearts and minds to not just understand and remember what Jesus taught, but to believe and obey it. He would illuminate all that had come before and they would finally see clearly who this Jesus of Nazareth was. The Spirit is still doing this work in us today.

It is the Spirit that moves, prompting our hearts to hear and respond to the gospel. He is the One who overwhelms us with our need for rescue from our sin and from ourselves. It's the Spirit in His work alongside Christ that caused the scales to fall from the eyes of Saul so that he might know the One He had been persecuting. He is the One who convicts us of our sin, shining His light into the dark recesses of our heart, exposing all the dirt we'd rather no one see. He is the One who moves us to righteousness, calling us to live as those who are walking in the Light, patterning our footsteps on the path of Jesus, the One who has gone before us who we do not see today, but will see so clearly when He returns.

The Spirit miraculously performs this work by illuminating the pages of Scripture, not as a weak reading light above a novel on a dark, chilly night, but like a lighthouse, issuing guidance and warnings through bright beams. He doesn't only help us truly see and understand God's Word, but He also gives us the power to obey. He is both lighthouse and wise captain as long as we step away from the wheel.

Your eyes cannot see without light, and without God revealing the truth about Jesus to you through the work of the Spirit, you cannot go from spiritual blindness to seeing. But when His light pours in through the illuminating work of the Spirit, you can't help but worship Him. Like a single candle in the deepest cave, even the smallest spark of the Spirit illuminates the dark cavern of our soul, bringing truth that requires a response: repentance, surrender, and worship. God has both revealed the truth and opened our eyes to it. It is only grace—only His work—that reconciles us with Him.

How did He call you to Himself? Seek to tell that beautiful story to someone who might need to hear it this week.

ADDITIONAL READING: Daniel 5:14; 1 Corinthians 2:10–16; 2 Corinthians 4:1–6

HIS POWER FOR
HIS PURPOSES

*"But you will receive power when the Holy Spirit has come
on you, and you will be my witnesses in Jerusalem, in all
Judea and Samaria, and to the ends of the earth."*

Acts 1:8

As a twelve-year-old, I felt called to ministry while at camp and begged
my friends not to tell my mom or our other leaders. I thought that a
call to ministry certainly meant I would move to Africa and never return,
and we had just lost my dad a few months earlier to cancer, so I was afraid
it would crush my mom to hear I was going to move away and never come
back. So, instead, I preferred threatening my friends over telling the truth
about what God was doing in my heart. Every invitation that mentioned a
call to ministry left me with my hands gripping the pew in front of me as
if I was riding a roller coaster and holding on for dear life, hoping this time
my commitment to keeping my feet still would work like it had for the ones
in the past. Eventually, God was moving so strongly that I could not continue to hide it. I had never seen God call women vocationally to ministry
unless they were missionaries, but that didn't seem like what He was calling

me to do. Yet, I committed to go or do whatever He asked. As I got older, I was exposed to women using their specific gifts in ways I didn't expect, and much to my mom's relief (and my own), I found that I could use the gifts I had been given to serve God without needing to cultivate a whole host of new skills I would need if He was truly calling me to the mission field.

In hindsight, after much growth, I know God would have equipped me for any calling—but it is such a joy to get to serve Him with teaching and writing today. And yet, He could call me to a new assignment tomorrow across seas or the boundary of language and I know He would equip me for it. And whatever He calls you to, He'll equip you too. However, He won't equip us to the point that we feel as though we can rely on our own strength to complete His assignment. All kingdom work is miraculous and only possible with the power of the Spirit providing the words and strength needed to be witnesses to the good news of Jesus Christ in our community, city, state, nation, and world. You cannot do what He calls you to, but He can through you.

In the Old Testament, we see the Spirit at work among judges, prophets, priests, and kings. He gave prophets supernatural power to take messages of judgment from God to people and proclaim the good news of a coming Messiah who would take away the sins of the world. He empowered judges and kings to rule as He intended and spoke powerfully to and through priests. He was active and engaged in opening the eyes of those who trusted God's promised Messiah.

In the New Testament, the Spirit falls in a greater portion to His people at Pentecost in Acts 2, shortly after Jesus gave His disciples this promise in Acts 1:8 and just before He ascended into heaven. And immediately, the gospel went forth miraculously, both in Jerusalem and in all the world. At Pentecost alone, three thousand people came to know the Lord, and in the months and years that followed, the gospel would be taken into Asia and Europe. The common denominator of it all is the Spirit's work of empowering God's people to do God's work. He sent them out into Jerusalem, Judea, Samaria, and the ends of the earth, guided by the whispers of the Spirit, empowered to go bravely, and emboldened with the right words—His words. He allows us to join Him in this mission and also rightly equips us to do it. God is achieving His mission through the work of His Spirit; you must only be a willing vessel—a clay pot ready for filling so that you may pour out your life for the cause of the gospel.

What is God calling you to do that seems too big? Imagine Paul's call to traverse the Mediterranean, facing shipwreck, imprisonment, and likely death. Only through the power of the Spirit can God's people do His work, and with Him all things are possible. May the Potter, who prepares, cares for, and directs, be glorified as He empowers you. How do you need to surrender to His call to obey today, even if that means you might be broken or cracked in the process?

ADDITIONAL READING: Colossians 1:11; Ephesians 3:14–21

AN ADVOCATE WHO TEACHES

"But the Advocate, the Holy Spirit, whom the Father
will send in my name, will teach you all things and
will remind you of everything I have said to you."
John 14:26 NIV

My husband loves to listen to true crime podcasts while he drives, but I won't let him when I'm in the car because I'm not looking to add to my list of possible nightmares. Not only are the crimes terrifying, but so are the heated courtroom arguments. I already relive my one traffic court experience where I was so nervous before the judge that my hands were shaking. That speeding ticket and the resulting "plea" rightly landed me in traffic school. My husband and so many others like him live for the back-and-forth in the courtroom and all the details of the case. In recent years, interest has grown so much that it's become a cottage industry with websites and podcasts wholly committed to detailing new cases and even bringing forth old ones to be reexamined. While I don't love the genre of true crime, I do know that the outcome of the case can be significantly influenced by the competency of the advocate. Every defendant deserves an attorney who understands the law, the judge's expectations, and the case.

We have an Advocate who is not only defense attorney, advocating before the Father on our behalf, but He also is Himself God. This Advocate is also Judge. The word translated "Advocate" here is *Paraclete*. This word may also be translated as "Comforter" or "Helper," reminding us not just of His work of mediation, but also the care with which He does so. He is sent from the Father and Son, intent upon teaching and reminding His people of the message of Christ. Because we are a forgetful people, aren't we? Thankfully, we have an Advocate who knows, and is consistent with His gentle reminders, and when we forget, He never fails to continue advocating for us before the Father, pointing to our unity in Christ's body and the conferred righteousness we have received on His behalf. He doesn't advocate based on our own rights or accomplishments, but on the finished work of Christ that covers our sin and brings victory over death.

Jesus said this of the Spirit, who is this Advocate: "When he comes, he will convict the world about sin, righteousness, and judgment" (John 16:8). He is both an Advocate full of gentle reminders, and a corrective Advocate who teaches all things Jesus has said, calling out our sin and reminding us of the already applied righteousness that we have through Jesus that we also must live. While His correction may feel sharp, it is certainly a comfort, as there is no better place to be than to be right with God and in the center of His will.

The Spirit teaches us by illuminating God's Word for us, helping us understand what we are incapable of understanding without Him. He acts as a Mediator not only for us before God but for God before us, mediating His Word to the recesses of our hearts that need it so desperately and intervening for us before God, proclaiming our innocence before the perfect Judge due to Jesus's perfect life, death, resurrection, and ascension into which we are united.

The Spirit is the applier of God's grace to us, opening our eyes to our need for our desperate rescue. He is the Sustainer, holding us in Christ as

Christ holds to us, sealing us until the new heaven and new earth we long for are reality. He's more than a lawyer in the courtroom of heaven. He's also God within us, advocating within, beseeching us to live a life worthy of the calling of Christ.

He stands with us. He dwells within us. He stands before the Father for us. This is the gift of the Spirit—we do not advocate for ourselves, but He advocates for us; and He does not advocate from our account, but from the blameless account of Christ. You do not need to fear standing before the Judge, because your case has already been settled.

ADDITIONAL READING: John 14:16–17; John 16:7; Romans 8:26

GOD WHO PERSEVERES THROUGH US

Now it is God who strengthens us together with you in Christ,
and who has anointed us. He has also put his seal on us and
given us the Spirit in our hearts as a down payment.
2 Corinthians 1:21–22

In the ancient Near East, letters were often sent from king to king via messenger. To ensure that the letter had not been tampered with, the king would seal the letter with hot wax, pressed with his signet ring. From the seal, all would know who had sent the letter. The seal acted as his signature. You are like a letter in the hand of God; His seal testifies to whom you belong. This seal can only be opened by the One to whom you are promised, the One who will welcome you home in the new heaven and new earth.

Seals were also used on wineskins or bottles of wine, and a broken seal would make it obvious the wine was not safe to drink. A broken seal could mean that the wine is spoiled, or even that it had been poisoned. This seal had a purpose, preserving the wine for when it was to be poured out. You are like the wine awaiting to be poured out at the wedding feast of the Lamb, sealed with the Spirit, secure in His care.

Down payments secure a home in the homeowner's possession with the promise of completing the lien, paying in full over time. This is the promise of the Spirit: He is securing us for a future, allowing us to experience His presence in part today, but in full upon completion, when the fullness of time comes. His sealing doesn't mean that we won't fail, we won't doubt, we won't stray. But it does mean that He will lovingly bring you back, replacing your failure with His righteousness and your doubt with His peace.

The Enemy is hard at work, seeking to lure you away or lull you into complacency, either seeding doubt as he did with Eve or fueling an appetite for sloth in the things of God: less focus, dwindling communion, an indifference toward His people and His mission of bringing the good news to the world. If he can't convince you to doubt what you believe, he's hoping he can convince you to ignore it in the way you live. But you have been redeemed. You have been rescued from this, and the Spirit holds you in this rescue. He holds you in the truth as the seal and down payment of what is to come. He is persevering through you, even when you feel as though you cannot persevere yourself. You are sealed.

And who better than to be our seal than the ever-present, ever-working Spirit who is not simply with us, but within us? He does not only teach us the truth so that our ears may hear and our minds may understand, but so that our heart may love. He is not a God who is far away, giving orders but never engaging in a relationship. He is near—nearer than the breath that fills your lungs or the blood that fills your veins. While there will be seasons that likely feel distant, we rest in His sealing—that the seal has not been broken; that we are full of purpose, preserved for the coming glory of God; and that we live as those who have already received a portion of our inheritance, even now, in the presence of the Spirit.

When you struggle to push on, God will persevere through you. When you yearn for His return, so ready to trade in the messes of this world for the order and glory of the next, God will continue to hold you in His hand, allowing you to feel the tragedies of the world, but not allowing them to pull you from it. Like a letter in the hand of a king, we await the day when these seals will be broken and we will see Him face-to-face, but until then, we hold tight to the Spirit who indwells us, as He holds tight to us.

You have no reason to fear. You are held. You are sealed. You hold the down payment that is a sure promise that the fullness of His glory is but a short wait away. Wait well today. Trust well today. Stand well today.

ADDITIONAL READING: 2 Corinthians 1:21–22; 2 Corinthians 5:5; Ephesians 1:13–14

MORE NEAR THAN THE HEART THAT BEATS INSIDE YOUR CHEST

But as for me, God's presence is my good.
I have made the Lord GOD my refuge,
so I can tell about all you do.
Psalm 73:28

When my kids were small, they often asked why we had lots of people over, but never asked God to come eat dinner with us. After all, we had enough chairs around the table to add Him to our seating arrangement, and if He was as close as we say He is, then it shouldn't be a difficult drive. And if He wants us to know Him like we had said that He does, of course, He'd be open to eating at our house and chatting so we could ask Him questions and get to know Him more.

Yet God is not like a dinner guest who comes and goes. Interacting with the Trinity is not like interacting with the human guests that we serve at our table, because He is ontologically different from us. And because He is different from us, our way of knowing Him is also different from the way we know others. Because He is so different, He took on flesh so we might know Him in ways our mental faculties could handle. Two millennia ago, across a narrow three decades, you could invite God over for dinner, and while I find myself wishing I had the opportunity to walk and talk with Jesus before His ascension, He said the Spirit's presence in our lives would be even better.

So if Jesus ascended into heaven, where is He now? And where exactly is heaven—geographically or spatially speaking? I don't have easy answers for these questions, but I know Scripture says He sits (or stands, as in Acts 7:55–56) at the right hand of the Father in heaven—an expression of His equal status with God (Col. 3:1; Heb. 1:3). Yet He is outside of our understandings of space and time, able to both sit at the right hand of the Father and be ever-present in His world, just as He promised in His last words to His disciples: "And remember, I am with you always, to the end of the age" (Matt. 28:20b).

Jesus is with us through His Spirit and in His church. He is with us, both individually and as we gather together because we are His body, and He is with us to the same degree that we are "with" our arms or our kidneys. *With* is not even a strong enough preposition. He is closer than with us, through the Spirit, He is also *within* us. He hasn't just allowed us to ask questions and get to know Him or even to know Him in the pages of Scripture; He has given His Spirit to teach us when we do not even know what questions to ask.

Today, if you trust Jesus, the Spirit of the living God indwells you, uniting you to Christ. He has not left us to figure out how to trust Him or spend time in His presence on our own. Instead, He has drawn near, coming to us when we didn't know how to come to Him through Jesus and through the Spirit. He has drawn close since the very beginning, but today He is closer than the breath in our lungs or the blood in our veins. The One who walked with Adam and Eve in the garden, visited Sarah and Abraham, spoke to

Hagar, wrestled with Jacob, and spoke with Moses on Mt. Sinai is the One who has drawn near to us.

Psalm 139:7 says: "Where can I go to escape your Spirit? Where can I flee from your presence?" and David is rightly expressing the obvious answer. He goes on to say, "If I go up to heaven, you are there; if I make my bed in Sheol, you are there. If I fly on the wings of the dawn and settle down on the western horizon, even there your hand will lead me; your right hand will hold on to me" (vv. 8–10). There is nowhere we can go that God is not, and the greatest expression of His presence is found in His church; not a building that is occupied to worship Him a few times each week, but within His church, the people, the body of Christ. He meets with us as we open His Word together and commune with both Him and one another. The church should be the primary expression of the presence of God for a dark and dying world, a city on a hill and a light on a lamp stand. He is cultivating a piece of heaven in our midst, and it is found within the church. Do you feel distant from God? Spend time in His Word and with His church. Here is the goodness of His presence—the One who is closer than the heart that beats in our chest.

In Psalm 73:28, Asaph proclaims that God's presence is his "good," and I imagine if you were aware of how intimately involved in your everyday life that God truly is, you would proclaim the same. He is the very essence of good: its source, enactor, and enabler. His presence is our good.

ADDITIONAL READING: Psalm 16:11; Psalm 34:17–18; Philippians 4:4–5

DEATH TO LIFE

And if the Spirit of him who raised Jesus from the dead lives in
you, then he who raised Christ from the dead will also bring
your mortal bodies to life through his Spirit who lives in you.
Romans 8:11

The overarching story of the Bible is not God's plan and provision to pay the penalty we owed for our sin. There is certainly substitutionary work in the death of Christ, but to see this as the fullness of the gospel message cheapens His grace. Instead, the overarching story of the Bible is one of life that overcomes death—life that springs forth from death in resurrection because anything connected to God, the Source of life, cannot die. Jesus's death is not simply substitutionary atonement for sin, but resurrection from the dead. In our deadness to Him, we are bent toward sin, only able to act in our decay. But when we are found in Christ who is life, we are full of life, raised from the dead and now—instead of being dead to God and all His goodness—we are dead to sin and all its evil. This new birth is the picture of new life with God, reconciled into a right relationship with Him.

This death-to-life story is all over the Scriptures. The Spirit hovers over the void waters in the beginning before life springs forth and there's new life as God brings His people across the waters of the Jordan, making them a new people in a new land—both a sort of baptism signifying new life. Jesus is baptized as an example of what was to come for Him, beginning His ministry in the same way He would end it, by being buried with Him in death and raised to walk in newness of life (Rom. 6:4). He was raised to a new ministry, anointed for the work He was called to do that was imaged in the moment of His baptism. In this moment, His Sonship was proclaimed. Matthew 3:16–17 says it this way: "When Jesus was baptized, he went up immediately from the water. The heavens suddenly opened for him, and he saw the Spirit of God descending like a dove and coming down on him. And a voice from heaven said, 'This is my beloved Son, with whom I am well-pleased.'"

Jesus's baptism told this death-to-life story which He would later live out in His body at the crucifixion and resurrection, and this is the same resurrection that we will experience through the power of the Spirit—the same Spirit that raised Jesus from the dead. It is through the valley of death that God's people become as He intended—fully His with no hint of sin or decay, fully alive in Him. The early church fathers speak of death as the way to true humanity, with Christ's resurrected body as the example. Jesus has established a new covenant, a new definition of true life, true humanity, and He has invited us to join Him in this true life and true humanity through the work of the Spirit who unites us with Him. The Spirit who fell at Jesus's death to our sin and abundant life with Him through baptism and who raised Jesus from the dead is the same Spirit who opened your eyes to your need for a Savior, who called you to Jesus, and who continues to hold you sealed to Him. The Spirit of the living God who is all-present, all-powerful, and all-knowing dwells within you. He is not lesser or weaker than He was in Christ because He is a Person. He is either with you or absent, powerful or aloof. Now, His presence may be expressed or experienced differently because we are so committed to our sin, often loving it far more than we love the God who is with us, but He is unchanged from eternity past to the present. While our love for sin continues, His love for us is greater, progressively overpowering our wickedness and cultivating good.

This is the good news: Jesus rescued us not only from sin, but also from ourselves—our fleshly nature with its bent toward sin—with His death on the cross. We are dead to sin and ourselves and alive to Christ and His purposes, resurrected with Him to live an abundant life. From the moment of our salvation, we are living our eternal life with Christ, never to be apart from Him again, but we also await a resurrection that will come when Jesus returns and all who trust Him are raised to dwell with Him forever. Life can spring from death because of the power of the Spirit who also raised Christ. To be united to Him is to be connected to the Source of life, who gives it in its fullness—resurrecting life—to those who trust Him. This is the good news. You have been resurrected, and you await a final resurrection in which you will become like the resurrected Christ—the perfected Human—who will raise you as the same. You await a day when you will be fully and truly human with no hint of sin or decay, and it's sure, because Jesus has already achieved it.

ADDITIONAL READING: John 5:24; 1 Corinthians 15; Ephesians 2:1–10

INCOMPREHENSIBLE GRACE

For you are saved by grace through faith, and this is not from
yourselves; it is God's gift—not from works, so that no one can boast.
Ephesians 2:8–9

Grace often seems to be defined in our churches as a moment rather than the ongoing favor of God for His people. We talk about the grace given through Christ on the cross—saving grace—that is indeed the sweetest sound because it has saved wretches just like you and me. But we fail to talk about grace as the every-moment gift of God that extends all of God's blessing beyond His deserving, perfectly righteous Son to us wretches. It is His grace that has delivered us from the kingdom of darkness into His glorious kingdom of light. So yes, grace is found in the death and resurrection of Christ, but that is but the beginning. Because it would be more appropriate to say that grace *is* Jesus. He is the gift of God that has saved us through faith.

His grace is not synonymous with mercy, that generous gift of not receiving the fiery wrath we deserve. His patience and His care for all of creation, even those who do not and will not turn from their rebellion, are wrapped up in His mercy. But grace. Grace entered through the Son made

flesh and will persist until its completion in the New Jerusalem where we
will enjoy Him forever. Those rebelling against God experience His mercy,
but they will not experience His ultimate grace, this grace that is sufficient
for you and for me to secure us to the God we love, that provides all the
riches of Christ as we are united in Him, or in the language of Ephesians 1,
"every spiritual blessing in the heavens in Christ" (v. 3). Grace cannot be
earned, and at times it can feel like we unfairly won some sort of heavenly
raffle. It is both an indescribable gift and an incomprehensible mystery.

Grace doesn't make sense, this self-giving of God to the point of Jesus's
suffering so that we might live. It's a towering cathedral that employed generations in constructing the art of its marvels against the Western adoration
for utility and speed of productivity. It's God "giving us the shirt off His
back" after we kicked Him in the shin. It's lavish, only able to be received
and never reciprocated.

Biblical grace isn't a description of the gentleness with which God car-
ries Himself, as if He might relate to a delicate ballerina. Instead, biblical
grace is an aggressive outpouring of God's kindness; a right-siding of an
upside-down world that leaves us a bit seasick; an uprooting of our old life
and a planting in an entirely new environment. Grace is uncomfortable,
because grace acknowledges our creatureliness, our need, our inability to
do good for ourselves. It's extravagant; a sinless Savior died, extending this
grace to us.

God has come. Grace has come. Grace is Christ. And God is full of
delight for you because of this grace, pouring out blessing after spiritual
blessing in Christ for you, if only you would humbly receive it. As high as
the heavens are from the earth—an unsearchable, incalculable distance—
is His love for His people. As far as the east is from the west—an infinite expanse—are the sins of His people removed. Psalm 103:8–14 details
this, closing with why God might be so gracious to us: He remembers us.
He remembers you. He knows that we are but dust, wholly reliant upon

a human-forming, dust-crafting Potter to make our lives into something redeemable; to make our lives overflow with His delight and blessing. All things bow at His command and may be used for His purpose, both in heaven and on earth, both those we can see and those we cannot. He holds all at His disposal, and in His grace, He gives us only blessing, only good from His hand. This good may look like crucifixion at times, but even then, our joy can bubble over because His grace given through Christ has saved us, is sustaining us, and will complete us when we are eternally in the fullness of His presence and grace—His riches for us.

This grace found John Newton in the middle of the Atlantic in 1748. He was a coarse sailor with a coarser mouth full of profanities who found himself in a violent storm, desperate that the sea would not swallow his boat whole. This wicked slave trader, whose hands were tethered to the boat's wheel so that he might maintain control in its tossing, remembered his God-fearing mother's earlier teaching and cried out, "Lord, have mercy on us!" Faced with what seemed like sure death, John would never be the same. He had cried out to God, and God had heard. When he finally returned to land, he never again went out to find and trade those he could capture, and he would later become an advocate against slave trade and a minister, just as his mother hoped.[46] This man, wretched, but found by God wrote these words in 1772:

> Amazing grace how sweet the sound
> That saved a wretch like me
> I once was lost, but now I'm found
> Was blind but now I see
> 'Twas grace that taught my heart to fear
> And grace my fears relieved
> How precious did that grace appear
> The hour I first believed.

Through many dangers, toils, and snares
I have already come
This grace that brought me safe thus far
And grace will lead me home.[47]

ADDITIONAL READING: Psalm 103:8–14; Isaiah 30:18; Romans 5:15; Jude 1:24–25

75

A GOOD JEALOUSY

"Do not make an idol for yourself, whether in the shape
of anything in the heavens above or on the earth below or
in the waters under the earth. Do not bow in worship to
them, and do not serve them; for I, the LORD your God,
am a jealous God, bringing the consequences of the fathers'
iniquity on the children to the third and fourth generations
of those who hate me, but showing faithful love to a thousand
generations of those who love me and keep my commands."
Exodus 20:4–6

Jealousy is a burning fire. I've seen it consume the peace and content-ment of many. It's burned down the beautiful memorials built for the brilliant moments in brilliant lives, comparison turning joy to bitterness. Jealousy is an ugly evil in the hands of humanity, but it is a beautiful gift in the hands of a holy God.

Our God is not jealous like you or I are jealous—a burning glare toward the one who holds what we cannot, wishing our lives were different in a number of ways so that we might finally be fulfilled or happy or successful, or whatever marker of the good life we've chosen as our idol. This jealousy is laced with sin, lusting after the lives of our neighbor, often wishing ill upon them so that we might claw our way to the top, our ladder the backs of people we are called to love. This is a jealousy worthy of repentance, not a jealousy worthy of praise. God's jealousy also burns like a consuming fire, but this is a purified, hot fire. This jealousy does not wish his life different but wishes our lives different for our own good and His own glory. His jealousy is not a self-seeking jealousy that comes at the expense of others, but a glory-seeking jealousy that benefits all who get to participate in it.

This jealousy topples idols and removes the traps we set for ourselves that deceive our hearts but delight our flesh. God will not be second in our lives. His jealousy simply will not allow it. He will not stop until He has uprooted whatever is prized above Him, crushing our idols beneath His feet. And this is for our good. Our commitment to our idols is synonymous with choosing to live in a tent in the rain rather than the glorious palace of a King, convinced that it is truly better for us that way. We live intent upon convincing ourselves that the tent is actually the glorious and the palace is the imitation. How silly our idols look to the only living God! It is for our good that He commands us "do not make an idol for yourself." John Calvin called our hearts idol factories,[48] and the factory powers up every time we take our eyes off of Jesus as King. This is the pattern of the Israelites: the moment they stopped pursuing the ways of God, they found themselves worshipping something that could not hear or help them. But God will not be found as one among many gods; He is the only God, jealous for His people.

One of my favorite shows of God's jealousy in the Scriptures is found in 1 Samuel 5. God's people had done just what Exodus 20:4–6 warned them not to do. They were living lives of idolatry, content to be separated from God's presence as long as they could continue in their wicked ways. The ark of the covenant—the place of God's presence—is taken by the Philistines and placed in the temple of their god, Dagon. Across two consecutive mornings, God prostrated Dagon before Him, testifying to the God of Israel as the One true God. The second morning, Dagon's head and hands were broken off beside him on the ground. Dagon could not put himself together, hear their prayers, or meet their needs. And the God of Israel revealed His sovereignty over the god of the Philistines. He cannot be in the presence of these false gods that we serve without crushing them, because they are just pieces of stone or metal or wood. They have no power and are nothing more than a fancy tchotchke found in your grandmother's collection of yard sale treasures.

The powerful presence of God crushes the idols in His presence, and this is good, because if they were not crushed, we would be. For His good and glory, and because of His jealousy, it is better that we be crushed so that we may turn away from our idols than for us to continue in rebellion.

Our God is a jealous God—jealous for glory, praise, and for His people to serve Him, because it is in serving Him that they flourish.

What idol of your heart must you crush today? Knock it off the high places of your heart. Your God will not share a platform. He is not one among many; He is the only One, sovereign over all, incomparable in all His ways. May His jealousy consume anything you are trusting that is not Him today.

ADDITIONAL READING: Exodus 34:14; Deuteronomy 4:23–24; Psalm 78:58; 2 Corinthians 11:2

76

A GENTLE LEADER
WITH AN EASY YOKE

"Come to me, all who labor and are heavy laden, and I will
give you rest. Take my yoke upon you, and learn from me,
for I am gentle and lowly in heart, and you will find rest for
your souls. For my yoke is easy, and my burden is light."
Matthew 11:28–30 ESV

Like a father who holds His child's hand as they learn to walk and rocks
them to sleep at night, God is gentle with us. This picture of gentleness
is not weakness or fragility. It's not even a preparatory gentleness, as though
His care was for the purpose of us one day not needing it like a parent seeking to launch a child into adulthood. Instead, this gentleness is a restrained
power; a conscious bearing of weight so that another can bear less, not in a
fleeting moment, but in every moment. His power and holiness could crush
us, but instead, He meets us gently, carrying in Christ what we could not
hold. This bearing of weight has released us from its pressure, allowing us
true rest.

Are you carrying the weight of the world on your shoulders? Trade
yokes with the Savior, who has borne the weight of our sin and rebellion on

His shoulders and given us His yoke of freedom and righteousness, a yoke that is light because it lacks the unliftable baggage of sin and death. He is gentle and lowly, approachable in every way. Not that He does not share in the Father's holiness, a holiness that the angels proclaim and that requires a heavy veil of separation in the temple. He is holy, but He is also gentle, inviting us to come to Him and lay down our burdens at His feet so that He may do something about them. He already has done something about them, but we do not enjoy that finished work until we relinquish control ourselves. So often, we want to hang on to our yoke, maybe we like the wounds etched into our shoulders by its harness or the sin and guilt that make it too heavy to wear, bending us down in its constant pressure.

The gentleness of Christ is like an unsnapping of the gear, a laying-down of the heaviness of what we carry, knowing we never have to pick it back up again. It's a fling-open-the-door-and-welcome-you-home kind of gentleness that doesn't keep an account of wrongs. This is a gentleness that does not bristle at the idea of taking on the weight of the sin that you intentionally choose to carry, but that finds great joy in the look of relief in your face. God is gentle, carefully unhooking each piece of the yoke we've chosen, deliberately and skillfully for your greatest good. He did not take on flesh and take on the role of a powerful monarch, ruling with an iron fist. He took on the form of a servant, rather than being served. He comes riding on a young donkey, not a majestic horse (Zech. 9:9) because He is gentle and humble, the Lamb of God.

Gentleness is clearly displayed in Christ, and what we see in Christ we know is true of the Godhead. God is patient with Israel, pointing to the coming Messiah and guiding them gently through His Spirit. The triune God is not harsh toward His people, but even in His disciplining and judgment, He is restrained. We are not treated as those who are simply servants, but as children and heirs alongside Christ. He is gentle, bringing rest for our weary souls.

Are you weary? Take off that yoke, despite the way it has carved troughs in your skin. Despite the familiar fit. Despite the way your muscles have sought to compensate for its awkward shape. Despite the many times you've laid it down and come back to get it, subjecting yourself to its weight again. Come to Jesus. Lay down your striving and your attempts to be good enough in your own doing. Lay down your failures, but also your triumphs. The world piles on, but Jesus sets free. His yoke is easy and His burden is light, and He welcomes you with a gentle and humble heart. Come and rest.

ADDITIONAL READING: Psalm 18:35; Isaiah 40:11; James 3:17

OVERFLOWING HOPE

Now may the God of hope fill you with all joy
and peace as you believe so that you may overflow
with hope by the power of the Holy Spirit.
Romans 15:13

I magine leaving for a short fishing trip in November, only to not return until fourteen months later. A storm rolled in two days into this fishing trip for Salvador Alvarenga, tossing his little boat around. He was an experienced captain, but before setting off on the trip, he noticed there was no anchor. Not considering a coming storm and knowing it was a short trip, he thought he could rely on his experience instead of having a need for an anchor, but being unable to drop a heavy anchor into the seabed caused his boat to be blown farther and farther from the land. Eventually, his first mate that made the journey with him succumbed to the difficulty, breathing his last on the boat. Alvarenga experienced deep despair, grieving for his friend and believing his next destination was heaven. It was 438 days before he washed ashore in the Marshall Islands.[49] What great loss, experienced because of a litany of issues, but most of all, the lack of an appropriate anchor.

Anchors have been used since ancient times to stabilize a boat in the sea. Its metal tines dig into the seabed, keeping the boat tethered in one place and combatting the raging seas when a storm approaches. An anchor is a small tool attached to a smaller, long, skinny chain, and yet, it often holds the difference between shipwreck and safe return in its use.

Hebrews 6:19 calls our hope the anchor of our souls.

Misplaced hope in the things of this world will reveal an anchor that cannot hold; a life beaten by the waves and capsized by the enormity of the challenges you face. Anchors bring security, but hoping that your achievements or success (or your children's), financial security, or good health will hold in the pressures of your life is likely to plunge you into the icy waters of despair.

And yet, hope in Christ—the only hope that holds—is the source of joy and peace, and it overflows in us because God is a God of hope. To trust Him is to receive this gift of hope from Him to the point of overflowing. True hope can only be found in Him because He is the well from which it is drawn, the One who has eternally been full of hope, giving it freely to His people as it flows from His character.

True hope both looks back at the faithfulness of God to do as He says He will do and looks forward to the future, trusting that He will make all things come to pass as He says. Hope is staked only on the character and promises of God, and it is an anchor that holds in the roughest seas. It is through the power of the Spirit, who has opened our eyes to the hope found in being dead in sin and alive with Christ, and it is the hope of sure resurrection, just as our Savior has been resurrected.

Hope lives as though we are in a cosmic rehearsal for Jesus's return, staking its stability on the eternal reign of Christ rather than focusing on the seemingly continual storms in your life. Those are but for a moment—a vapor—compared to the promise of forever. Our hope looks forward, knowing that the Spirit is the down payment of what is to come, confirming its truth. We believe. May we be filled with joy and peace as we actively hope in Christ, filled by God to the point of overflowing. He is an anchor that will hold.

ADDITIONAL READING: Psalm 33:20–22; Isaiah 40:31; Romans 8:24–25; Colossians 1:27; Hebrews 10:23

78

HE WILL FIGHT FOR YOU

*"For the LORD your God is the one who goes with you to
fight for you against your enemies to give you victory."*
Deuteronomy 20:4

I go out of my way to make as few enemies as possible in life. Just taking
the trash out in the dark causes me to do a lot of looking over my shoulder, afraid of being eaten by the not-even-there local wild life in my very
populated neighborhood off a busy road. And I spend enough time staring
at the ceiling in the middle of the night wondering if the crossing guard who
yelled at me for not stopping far enough back as a sixteen-year-old driver
still hates me. Conflict avoidance is my way of life; it's the only functional
enemy I'm comfortable having.

But live long enough, and you'll find not everyone is as committed to
world peace as beauty pageants on TV led you to believe. Some people love
conflict, even unnecessary conflict. No amount of monitoring the feelings
of others or de-escalation can make the way easy. The thorny underbrush
of envy, anger, distrust, and disgust are sure to catch your feet. Whether
by your sin or another's, or whether it is only by Adam's, sin has disrupted
God's peace. The Enemy who met Eve in the garden, sowing lies in her

heart and deception in her ear, also sprouted thorny vines that would wrap around that heart, entangling her, and even at times, causing confusion over if the pricks of the vine are pricks from him or from the Spirit. We have an Enemy, whether we try with all we have to avoid it or not. Our Enemy is not of flesh and blood (Eph. 6:12); your battle is not of this world. The world of darkness fights for your attention and would love for you to succumb to its attempts at throwing you into confusion and chaos. This is the war you are in. The wars that seem to steal all your attention as you engage in battle with other image-bearers are a distraction from the true warfare you are meant to fight.

Whether fruit or thorns, the growth of the ground is due to the cultivation of another. The thorny vine grows furiously, even in the dark, ready to wrap you in its power and put your face in the dirt when your feet fail you. Your Enemy would rather you dead, the breath removed from your lungs as his powerful vines constrict around your heart. But it isn't your face that God banished to the dirt, to crawl around on your belly. No one likes to fall alone, and he'll take as many with him as he can collect.

But his power is only weakness compared to the power of the One who holds us in His hand, who makes straight our paths, clearing away the thorny vine by taking it upon Himself, by wearing it as a crown of thorns, descending into the depths of the pit and rising victorious. Yes, God fights for us before our enemies just as He did for His people in Deuteronomy. The odds were almost always stacked against them. They'd have far less men than the opposing armies, and yet, when God was with them, they were victorious. When God was with them, the sun stood still (Josh. 10:12). When God was with them, He told them they must only be still (Exod. 14:14). This God of victory, the Lord of Armies, is undefeated in His interventions. He does not attempt and fail. The Enemy may seem to have a stronghold. He may seem a valiant warrior. It may seem his vines have so flourished in our hearts that even God cannot clear the way, but the Enemy won't prevail.

God is a master gardener, and the Enemy's power looks like extreme weakness in light of God's power.

Are the vines grasping at your ankles? Don't forget to look down and see if your feet have wandered from God's path. God's people didn't win every battle, but it's not because God was overpowered or dismayed. He uses even our stumbles, scratches, and wounds for our good. He uses them for our ultimate victory, moving us to deeper trust of the One who fights for us as we learn to know and love Him. We learn to be still. Sometimes, we need to be carried, and we serve a God who will do just that. He fights for us. He fights for you. You are not alone or unseen or undefended. Though enemies may rise against you, your God will fight for you. You do have an Enemy, but he has already been defeated. He may haunt you in the dark today, but for all of eternity, there is only light. Come out into the light. His vines can't grow there.

ADDITIONAL READING: Genesis 3:15; Romans 16:20; Ephesians 6:10–12; Revelation 20:10

79

OUR GOD IS A CONSUMING FIRE

Therefore, since we are receiving a kingdom that cannot be
shaken, let us be thankful. By it, we may serve God acceptably,
with reverence and awe, for our God is a consuming fire.
Hebrews 12:28–29

Fire warms, brings light, and purifies, and it is the key indicator of survival if you find yourself lost on a deserted island. Water is boiled to the point of it being made clean, food is cooked to the point of removing parasites or bacteria, light provides protection from the beasts that roam in the dark, and the glow of burning embers emits heat that warms even in the coldest night in the wilderness. It purifies and forges metal, hardens glazed pottery, and has the ability to burn an entire forest in a matter of hours with the right wind. It can be uncontrollable and destructive, or carefully built and stoked.

God shows up in fire for His people, its roaring blaze an image of His holiness and glory. He speaks to Moses through a burning bush (Exod. 3) that was on fire but not burned up. It was a spectacle unlike any that had been seen before. This bush was on fire but not consumed because God's presence had made it holy ground. That which is holy blazes but is not consumed, like choice metal without impurities.

Unlike the burning bush, the fire at the temple's altar consumed every offering. This fire was to be continually burning (Lev. 6:12–13), and when the temple was dedicated, fire rained down from the presence of the Lord and consumed the offering (Lev. 9:24). So while the priests kept it going, the Lord brought the initial fire. This fire completely consumed the offering given for the forgiveness of sin, proving that our God is both alive—able to consume it—and that the offering was accepted, providing the forgiveness of sin because the animal's life covers the life of the guilty. He consumes all that is not pure, consuming the offerings that represented the people's sin. This is also why the three men thrown into the fiery pit by King Nebuchadnezzar were not burned up (Dan. 3:23–30). While this is not the fire of altar, the One who was in the fire with them made the space holy, and nothing that is holy is consumed by fire because it is already purified.

We should approach Him with awe and reverence because He is an uncontrollable, all-consuming fire, intent upon consuming all that is wicked or sinful. This consuming is not for the purpose of destruction, like a wildfire, but for our good, even when it seems His fire brings desolation to the places we've been cultivating that do not honor Him. He is committed to our purification, even when it means experiencing the fire of adversity. And for our greatest good, God has given us the Spirit who was seen as flaming tongues of fire in Acts 2:1–4 to purify us from within.

He purifies our hearts and levels idols, turning anything that is not eternal to ash. His burning glory consumes all, contains all. He purifies that which is already valuable and burns up the chaff. He is awe-worthy, like a kid standing before a bonfire ten times larger than them, amazed by the raging sound of its glory, the uncontrollable flame that consumes all it touches, and the unbelievable heat.

We cannot know the true God—the consuming fire—and not come back smelling like fumes. His purification is transformative—noticeable—moving us to be wholly consumed with His purposes and His will. We cannot stand before the blaze of His glory without falling to our faces in worship because of His greatness. Our God is an overwhelming, all-consuming, weight-bearing, attention-keeping fire. How is He purifying you today? How do you see His light and feel His heat?

ADDITIONAL READING: Exodus 3:2–3; Exodus 40:38; Numbers 9:15–16; Daniel 7:9; Revelation 19:12–13

WHEN WRATH IS GOOD

The LORD is a jealous and avenging God;
the LORD takes vengeance
and is fierce in wrath.
The LORD takes vengeance against his foes;
he is furious with his enemies.
The LORD is slow to anger but great in power;
the LORD will never leave the guilty unpunished.
His path is in the whirlwind and storm,
and clouds are the dust beneath his feet.
Nahum 1:2–3

In earlier years of walking with Christ, I preferred to skip over God's wrath and move on to more "positive" truths about God like His love or His grace. That a God so full of gentleness and compassion would also hold wrath seemed to be a contradiction I couldn't grasp, so instead of seeking understanding, I'd just gloss over thoughts or conversations about His wrath on the way to what I considered better truths about Him. In *Delighting in the Trinity*, Michael Reeves quotes theologian Miroslav Volf, who felt similarly to me (and likely you) about God's wrath until he lived through the brutalities of a war in former Yugoslavia. This beloved place of his was destroyed and more than 200,000 people were killed. Volf said, "I could not imagine God not being angry. . . . Though I used to complain about the indecency of the idea of God's wrath, I came to think that I would have to rebel against a God who wasn't wrathful at the sight of the world's evil. God isn't wrathful in spite of being love. God is wrathful because God is love."[50] In the passage above, God promises judgment for Nineveh, the hub of the cruelty of the Assyrian Empire. This empire has terrorized the ancient Near East, overtaking and enslaving nations. While this message seems harsh, it was also good and right. Kenneth Barker said it this way: "To the people of Nahum's day, his message was one of comfort and deliverance of oppressed people. For the oppressed to be freed, the oppressor had to be removed. Nahum spoke about the end of the oppressor, Nineveh."[51]

There is no end to the world's brutal atrocities on this side of eternity, and in love, God's anger burns against the oppressors of righteousness and justice. God does not respond with ambivalence to the desecration of His image by the oppressed. God does not stand idly by. He is not a distant God, unaware and inactive. His wrath is stirred up when His justice is perverted by the unjust, correcting wrongs.

It's easy to be thankful for God's wrath when it is upon the heads of the evil, but what about when it's directed toward us? Ephesians 2:3 explains that by nature, we are children of wrath. We are bent toward injustice and away from obedience to God's righteous instructions. In our sinful nature, we are focused only on ourselves, unphased by the suffering of others. God's wrath is upon us because we are disobedient (John 3:36). He has given us over to our "dishonorable passions" (Rom. 1:26 ESV)—our own path of destruction.

For us, the children of wrath oppressed by sin and unable to obey God rightly because of the inherited sin nature given to us by Adam, God also made a way for the oppressor to be removed. On the cross, the wrath of God was poured out on Jesus, who absorbed every drop that we deserved. There's now no condemnation for those in Christ, and we are adopted from our family of origin—wrath—to the family of God who brings wholeness. It's in Christ that we find shielding from His wrath, brought in as those who have received Jesus's applied account, His holiness freely given to us. Even God's wrath is a gift for those who are in Christ, flowing from His righteousness and justice and only landing upon those in rebellion to His ways. He is jealous for His people, never leaving the guilty unpunished, but also satisfying that guilt in the life and death of Christ, who bore it for us. He is bringing justice in all things, and justice for us is good.

ADDITIONAL READING: Psalm 7:11; Obadiah 1:15; John 3:36; Romans 1:18; Revelation 19:11–21

NEVER TIRED

Do you not know?
Have you not heard?
The LORD is the everlasting God,
the Creator of the whole earth.
He never becomes faint or weary;
there is no limit to his understanding.
Isaiah 40:28

I've lived the last eight years of my life tired. We brought home two babies—one through the gift of adoption and one through the gift of biology—just four months apart, and while there was more joy than our little house could contain, there was also more exhaustion (and baby spit-up) than I've ever experienced. I went about five years without sleeping through the night, and then when we thought we might finally lose the bags under our eyes, we brought home our youngest. Again, the joy made our hearts light and the eyelids heavy.

What keeps you up at night? Not the nights that the thunderstorm throws the kids (and the dog) tossing and turning into your bed, but the days you toss and turn, unable to release the plaguing anxiety? What takes your mind on a never-ending carousel of worry? What ghost of seasons past haunts your thoughts, given far more play time on the screen in your mind than deserved, despite the "not worth your time" review you give it each time in a personal pep talk?

While there is no end to our exhaustion, there is no end to his capacity. He is neither limited by biology or by restlessness. He neither tires nor does He tire of you. His understanding is infinite;: there is no anxiety in Him over neither past nor future, no fear of falling victim to a world where He has no control because He is sovereign Lord over all. He never ceases to act for His people, He never misses a moment because He is out of the office, and He is never caught unaware.

This is why the Christian can enjoy unexplainable rest, no matter the exhaustion of our days or the spinning of our minds. God is not simply a God who does not sleep, as if insomnia has taken hold and He is seeking entertainment to fill His time. He is a God who does not tire of doing good; He is unstoppable in His advocation for His people and His moving forward with His kingdom purposes. He is not thwarted in any of His ways. Like a fast-moving, never-pausing, city-to-city lightning rail, He is moving in a singular direction toward the fulfillment of history—a train whose destination is the eternal good of His people found in the eternal light of His face in the new heavens and new earth.

Because God does not sleep and is not surprised by a single instance in the expanse of our days, we can truly rest, not holding tightly to what we desperately seek to control, but releasing all that holds us back from true rest—mind, body, and spirit—to the One who can and already does carry it all. We are more like drowsy, nonsensical copilots on a fiercely long road trip, truly believing we are helping the driver make every turn, when we should truly just go to sleep. Maybe the most spiritual thing you should do today is sleep. Not as an escape, but as a testimony of a deep trust that you are not truly holding the earth on its axis, despite it feeling as though it might roll right off if you relax. While you sleep, He continues to hold the sun and the stars in His hand. While you sleep, He continues to place the tracks for the next second on the clock. He does not tire and He is only good. You can rest. You can sleep, even if chaos is swirling. Trust Him.

Augustine said it well in this beautiful quote from his *Confessions*, speaking of God:

> You have made us for yourself, and our hearts are
> restless, until they can find rest in you.[52]

Because He does not rest, you can.

ADDITIONAL READING: Psalm 121:3–4; Jeremiah 31:26; Matthew 11:28

HAVE I SEEN THE ONE WHO SEES ME?

*So she named the L*ORD *who spoke to her: "You are El-roi," for she said, "In this place, have I actually seen the one who sees me?"*
Genesis 16:13

Hagar experienced great turmoil as the result of another's sin. Because of such turmoil, I have a really hard time appreciating Sarai as an Old Testament matriarch. If I was doing the choosing, I don't think I'd choose Sarai to be such an important descendent in the lineage of Jesus and the matriarch of the people of Israel. Sarai was Abram's wife (later renamed Sarah and Abraham by God). They had left their home and traveled to a land God promised, settling there after many mishaps and mishandlings on their part. In this place of great promise, still, Sarai fumed over her inability to bear children. When she tired of waiting and thought that there was no way God could use her womb in her old age, she hatched a plan that went around God. She sent Hagar, her maidservant, to sleep with Abram, hoping that she would have a son and their lineage would continue through him. The plan worked, and Sarai burned with jealousy. Sarai was so mean to Hagar that she fled out into the wilderness, where there was no protection or provision. The wilderness is almost surely death for a woman like Hagar, pregnant and vulnerable, out in the barren wilderness of dangerous animals, dangerous people, and dangerous temperatures.

Yet, in Hagar's most vulnerable moment, God sees her suffering. In what continues to shock me, the angel of the Lord speaks to Hagar, and allows her to name God. The God who has not yet revealed Himself as I AM reveals Himself not to Abram or Sarai, chosen as His people, but to a servant in their house from a faraway land. Even in this moment, we see God's heart that Israel would be a light to the nations and that all might know and love Him. And in this moment where I want God to lead Hagar away forever, never to have to deal with suffering under the hands of angry Sarai, He sends her back home. He doesn't give her instructions to go somewhere new or build her a house and a way to have everything she needs right there in the wilderness. Instead, He tells her that she will have a son and that she is to return to what is already a hard situation, only sure to get harder as her belly begins to grow. And yet, she sees and names God. He is the God who sees, not as One who simply observes what is happening but who truly sees, knowing even the depths of the heartache within. While He doesn't remove her from her suffering, He sees it all and He cares, sure to continue on with her as she toils in this house of promise.

Jewish Midrash writings connect Hagar's entry into Abram and Sarai's home to their short stint in Egypt when there was famine in the land.[53] A big lie created quite a stir for the Pharaoh, and yet, they were gifted many things as they left. If this writing is true, Hagar went from needing nothing in the house of Pharaoh to suffering in the house of God's promise. She was alone and betrayed, desperate for another way as she fled into the dangerous wilderness alone. What should have been the most peace-filled life as one living within God's covenant family was full of sadness and mistreatment. Yet, God saw, and even more phenomenally, He allowed Hagar to know and name Him.

No matter what you face today, God sees. He is not unaware of your struggles, and He is also not inactive. While suffering comes for us all, we do not suffer alone because we serve a God who sees and knows, and He is in control of all, working it out for His purposes. He sees you. May we cast our eyes to Him so that He may allow us to see Him when we are walking in darkness too. I don't know why God doesn't remove us from our suffering immediately, but I know that His character is good and that He is aware and grieved by the trials and sadness of this world. He hates what sin has done to the world, both globally through its entry through Adam and Eve and in your family and your life.

There is a day that is coming when all sin and suffering and death will be no more, and until that day, we can rest in knowing that God sees. He will right wrongs. And He is with us. And He is good. Whether the suffering you face is a result of your sin, the sin of another, or the fallenness of all the world, God sees. Or maybe you are more like Sarai, embracing bitterness and stirring up trouble for another. He sees you, and He invites you to also see Him as the One who hasn't taken His eyes off of you. May you suffer well so that others may see the hope that is in you, no matter how difficult a road you walk.

ADDITIONAL READING: Proverbs 15:13; Isaiah 41:10; 1 Peter 3:12

HE HEARS

This is the confidence we have before him:
If we ask anything according to his will,
he hears us. And if we know that he hears whatever we ask,
we know that we have what we have asked of him.
1 John 5:14–15

Like a shepherd who knows the bleat of each of his sheep or a mom who recognizes her baby's cry in a nursery of half a dozen babies, God hears His children when they cry out to Him. God knows our every concern, and yet He has invited us to cry out to Him and He responds. This isn't like a message sent to a person on social media who you follow, but don't actually know and who doesn't actually know you. The odds are against you for that person reading your message, let alone responding to it.

Prayer is not cosmic email, as if you likely will wait twenty-four to forty-eight hours for a reply. It is also not a hotline for requests or even crises. Yes, God calls us to pray in these moments, but prayer is far more than an emergency call or a wish list. Prayer is not even synonymous with a chat with a friend over good food. No, prayer is the gift of God to His people for direct communion with Him. Prayer is like breathing, reflexive in nature and the very substance of our life with God.

It is in Jesus's prayers that we learn of God as Father—Abba—and in His prayer in the garden of Gethsemane that we learn what true surrender to His will looks like, as Jesus commits Himself to obedience even unto death. Jesus—who is God—consistently spent time in prayer with His Father, so how much more do we need this communion with Him, not only to be heard, but also to hear from Him? This is the reflexive nature of prayer, the speak and listen cadence required for true relationship, for true delight in the presence of God.

Through the work of the Spirit to unite us with Christ's life, death, resurrection, and ascension, our realest reality is in the presence of God. We are right with Him, given immediate access to Him without a priest or go-between because God Himself in Christ is our Mediator. He has made the way clear for us to never cease to pray, to never cease to be present in the throne room of God because we are united to Him. We don't have to go to a specific place to meet with God because, through Jesus's work on the cross, the veil in the temple was torn and the boundary lines of separation are dissolved.

You are invited to connect deeply with God through prayer, transferring your burdens to the only One strong enough to carry them all. You are invited to join God in what He is doing through prayer, and as you pray in His will, God acts.

He allows us to be a part of His mission—His kingdom, advancing plan—both nearby and afar through prayer. I don't understand all the logistics, but we know that prayer changes things. God hears and He moves when His people are walking in righteousness and call on His name. He withholds no good thing—none of His riches—from His children, and He rejoices in our requests because we are expressing our faith in Him as the One who has the power to change situations and because He loves to spend time with His children. How can you lean in to spending time in prayer with Him today? Consider this a beginning:

Lord, help me find joy and peace in meeting with You in Your presence, knowing You hear Your children and You respond within the good boundaries of Your will. Open my eyes to the beauty of prayer and the invitation to commune with You at any time and in any place. Meet with me here. Hear my requests and, if they fall within Your will, would You act? Make Your glory and Your presence known in the situations that have my attention and are pulling at my heart. . . .

ADDITIONAL READING: Psalm 34:15; Psalm 145:18; John 9:31; 1 Peter 3:12

HE HEARS AND HE ACTS

From ancient times no one has heard,
no one has listened to,
no eye has seen any God except you
who acts on behalf of the one who waits for him.
Isaiah 64:4

"Acts of God" don't just occur in insurance policies.

He brought about a great flood, delivered His people out of Egypt, made the sun stand still, and brought about locusts as judgment. When the ark of the covenant was placed in a pagan god's temple by the Philistines, He laid low their god, breaking him into pieces. He struck the Philistines with tumors and so much affliction that they packed up the ark and sent it away, hoping it would go anywhere but back toward their land (1 Sam. 5–6). He held the sun still, sent a fish to deliver a prophet to Nineveh, and took on flesh, entering His world as a baby laid in a manger.

God didn't just create all things, but He also sustains all things, actively involved in the everyday lives of His people, acting on their behalf toward His purposes. And from ancient times, there has been no other God who is able to act, because the gods that are not Him do not live, hear, or act.

He is never inactive or sleeping, despite the moments we feel as though He isn't moving or isn't near. Our call is to wait on Him, knowing He hears and acts and that His timing is always perfect, even when it's far slower than we desire. Wait for Him. He will act for you. In Isaiah 64, God's people are crying out to Him from captivity, where waiting is a challenge. God's people desperately desire to go home, but they must wait. God is at work, hearing and acting, but part of that work is also facilitating the necessary learning while they are exiled. He heard and He answered, always in His intended timing.

Our God hears, sees, and acts. He is not made of stone or clay, unable to entertain our prayers. He is sovereign over all, able to command all things with His Word, and He cares. He acts in line with His character, always in love and justice. He has all things at His disposal: the heavens and the earth, the words of others, the situations we face. Nothing happens outside of His knowledge or in opposition to His intentions.

When you feel as though no one understands what you are walking through or as though nothing will ever be "good" again, remember this: You serve a God who acts, and all of His ways are love. You serve a God who loves so much that He sent His Son to take on flesh. He took on all the ailments of humanity, understanding them deeply. You are understood because God Himself has walked trials and suffering. Through Jesus's death on the cross, justice for your sin was secured. God's wrath was poured out on Jesus so that it would be fully absorbed by Him, not even a drop left for those who are in Christ. We trust He can and does act because He has. He has done great and glorious things for His people, and He continues today. Maybe you find yourself crying out for God to act today. I cannot promise He will do exactly what you hope, but I do know that He hears you and He acts, and that the greatest of these acts is His Son, which has secured His presence with you. His will may not be aligned with exactly what you are hoping, but you do not walk alone. He acts, both in the world and within the hearts and minds of His people even as we wait.

Choose to be wise in the way that you wait, like the wise women who brought extra oil for their lamps in case the waiting was a bit longer than they expected (Matt. 25:1–13) and the wise servants who invested the master's gold. They wisely planned for tangible proof of their waiting (Matt. 25:14–30). As Isaiah 64:4 says: God is the One "who acts on behalf of the one who waits for him." It's not always an easy wait. Sometimes the waiting lasts decades like for the woman with the problem of blood (Mark 5:25–34) and sometimes it lasts generations, like those exiled to Babylon in Daniel's time—the ones to whom the promise of Jeremiah 29:11 was given, but would not be fulfilled for another seventy years. God's timing is perfect, albeit often outside of our preferences. Waiting can be excruciating, but it can also be formative, helping us to become who we are to be as we wait for His return or as we wait for Him to act in response to our particular prayers. Don't give up praying. He's changing you in the waiting as He also changes situations. He is not idle. He will act, and He welcomes us to join Him in His acting through our prayers.

How do you need Him to act for you today? He knows and He hears. He has the power to act. You can trust Him.

ADDITIONAL READING: Psalm 18:6; Psalm 147:15–18; John 5:17; Philippians 2:13

SHIELDED ON EVERY SIDE

But you, LORD, are a shield around me,
my glory, and the one who lifts up my head.

Psalm 3:3

On July 17, 1505, a man was caught in a thunderstorm so intense that he promised God he would abandon his pursuit of law and instead study theology if only he could make it out alive. He narrowly avoided being struck by lightning, but was shielded from sudden death. And when the storm lifted, this young man did just as he promised. He abandoned law and instead became a monk and pursued studying theology.[54] This man, Martin Luther, would go on to bring about the Reformation, the catalyst from which evangelical faith may be traced. Not only did he write theological texts, he also wrote hymns, and one of the hymn's titles is inscribed upon his headstone.

This song, "A Mighty Fortress Is Our God" (based on Psalm 46), was written years after Luther was caught in the thunderstorm that changed the trajectory of his life, but it captures the truth of God being a safe place to hide, a good shield, a mighty fortress—precisely what he needed that day:

A mighty fortress is our God, a bulwark never failing;
Our helper he, amid the flood of mortal ills prevailing.
For still our ancient foe does seek to work us woe;
his craft and power are great, and armed with cruel hate,
on earth is not his equal.

And though this world, with devils filled, should threaten to
    undo us,
We will not fear, for God has willed his truth to triumph through us.
The prince of darkness grim, we tremble not for him;
His rage we can endure, for lo! his doom is sure;
One little word shall fell him.

—first and third verses

Sometimes we don't need someone to fight for us. Our situation is so bleak that offense isn't really on our minds. Instead, we need someone to shield us from the flaming arrows of the Enemy as they zoom toward us; someone to be our refuge in the storm. On this side of heaven, we are unaware of the multitude of interceptions God runs for us, stepping in to shield us from what could be, from what could destroy us. In David's case, he is writing Psalm 3 from a desperate place. Second Samuel 15–18 was playing out in real time. Until this moment, David, who was chosen by God as king, was beloved by his people. But in this passage, his son Absalom has turned the people against him, and David is fleeing for his life. Absalom wanted the power of the throne and did everything he could to overthrow David, seeking to kill him. Let that sink in. David's son was seeking to destroy him, which left him running into the wilderness to hide and pray for survival. Defeat seemed sure.

Yet, David will not be defeated because it is from him that Jesus will come—the King whose throne will never end. God holds an impenetrable shield over His chosen ones—and in this case, His chosen One. God's king-dom-bringing purpose cannot be thwarted.

God is both the One who fights for you and the One who is your shield. He will not allow the Enemy to overtake you or the flaming arrows to be fatal. He is your shield and your refuge. He may allow you to struggle and He may even allow you to be forced into the wilderness to hide (hopefully only metaphorically), but He will not allow you to be overtaken. He covers you with His protection, only allowing what He intends to pass.

When hardship comes, let us be quick to trust that He has delivered us from worse in the past, and He'll do it again. Even if the arrows of the Enemy do catch fire and take your physical life, no one can snatch you from the hand of God. This life is a vapor, but the life that He holds secure for you into eternity cannot be squelched and His plan cannot be thwarted.

Let the Psalms guide you to ask the hard questions of God. Cry out to Him in your need, but do not move out from under His protective shield. When the flaming arrows come, there is only one safe place. Rest in this: God is determin-ing your steps, but He is also sovereignly directing the footsteps of your enemy. He shields and He comforts. He shields and He directs. He shields and He loves. God is a shield, but what does it look like to stand under His protection? Martin Luther says it this way: "A fiery shield is God's Word; of more substance and purer than gold, which, tried in the fire, loses nought of its substance, but resists and overcomes all the fury of the fiery heat; even so, he that believes God's Word overcomes all, and remains secure everlastingly, against all misfortunes; for this shield fears nothing, neither hell nor the devil."[55]

ADDITIONAL READING: Genesis 15:1; Deuteronomy 33:29; Psalm 46; 2 Thessalonians 3:3

CAN YOU FATHOM
THE DEPTHS?

Can you fathom the depths of God
or discover the limits of the Almighty?
Job 11:7

Oh, the depths of the riches
and the wisdom and the knowledge of God!
How unsearchable his judgments
and untraceable his ways!
For who has known the mind of the Lord?
Or who has been his counselor?
And who has ever given to God,
that he should be repaid?
Romans 11:33–35

The lake I spent every summer of my childhood enjoying holds a city under its depths. In the early 1900s, a plan was made and the town of Kowaliga was alerted to evacuate. Over the coming weeks, the nearby dam would pump thousands of gallons of water into the town. Now more than one hundred years later, I rarely think about the city that lies below its depths, but it's a scuba diver's paradise. I've even heard that there are catfish the size of small vehicles hiding among the old structures. (This is the reason I prefer to stay in a boat or enjoy the lake from the land.) From the surface, you'd never imagine this lake's history, but the deeper you get, the more you find to explore. Similarly, the more we learn about God, the more we find that the depths are unable to be plumbed.

We know God only because He has revealed Himself to us in His Son, the Word made flesh, and while this self-revelation gives us what we need to know Him rightly, we do not yet know the extent of His depths. We cannot exhaust what we can know about Him on earth because there is always more to know, more to learn, and more reasons to worship.

Our finite minds that are being cultivated into resurrected infinite ones cannot yet grasp the fullness of who God is, what He has done, what He is doing, and what He will do. It's too beautiful. It's too expansive. We find the boundaries of our limitations as we ponder His immensity. He is in a category all His own. He is so different from us, so transcendent, that my brain, which works in drawing connections to what I know through the realities of this world, cannot piece together what I have not yet seen. It cannot understand that there is a reality coming that is more real than the elements I touch and see today, more concrete than the ground upon which we walk, and more vibrant than my gaze could absorb without being blinded by what my mind can only describe as unending light. The glimpses we catch of His glory on earth are enough for us to think on for the entirety of our lives; knowing that, even so, we only see dimly, just shadows of His radiance. We see in monochrome today but full color when He returns. A day is coming when we will not look as into a mirror dimly, but face-to-face, knowing not in part, but in full (1 Cor. 13:12).

He has shown us enough of Himself to find true salvation in Him—we know Him rightly—and one day we will fully know Him as He has always fully known us. His plans and movements are beyond our comprehension, sometimes causing us to question His goodness or His sovereignty, but we see only a sliver of history, only a moment of all He is doing. His ways are so much higher than our own. Even our lack of comprehension is for our good, as a God we can fully comprehend is no God at all. If we can fully comprehend all of His ways, then we should be God, not Him. He is gloriously incomprehensible, uncomplicated, but unfathomably infinite. Our limits just bring His limitlessness more into focus. We see only a glimmer of Him, a fingernail on the hand of a glorious God.

We allow the marvels of this world to take our breath away, and they do and they should because our redeemed eyes can see true things about our God in them, but they are only a shadow of who He truly is. Choose to explore His depths, knowing you don't have to be worried that a catfish will swallow you whole—Jonah-style—along the way. Instead, with every length deeper, His glory shines more brightly. His depths are unfathomable, and yet, He has revealed His love in His Son. Truth that the deeper we go, the more clearly we will see His goodness.

ADDITIONAL READING: Job 37:1–24; Ecclesiastes 3:11; Isaiah 40:12–13; 1 Corinthians 2:16

KNOWING AND LOVING GOD

*This is what the L*ORD *says:*
"The wise person should not boast in his wisdom;
the strong should not boast in his strength;
the wealthy should not boast in his wealth.
But the one who boasts should boast in this:
that he understands and knows me—
*that I am the L*ORD, *showing faithful love,*
justice, and righteousness on the earth,
for I delight in these things."
*This is the L*ORD'*s declaration.*
Jeremiah 9:23–24

What is true love? True knowledge? On the day I got engaged, I thought I understood what it meant to know and love another. On the day I got married, I realized that knowing and loving had continued to grow. Today, more than ten years later, I know I would not have been able to comprehend how knowing and loving my husband would increase over the years.

Can a God who is wholly other and distinct from us be truly known? Can He truly be both incomprehensible and known and loved? Comprehension and knowing are not synonymous. I knew my husband when I got engaged to him, but I did not yet comprehend every little thing, and still do not. I don't always know the precise reasons he chooses something new off a menu or a new hobby to chase, but still, I know him and I am learning him. Similarly, although of course not identical in nature, we do not know everything there is to know about God, but we know Him because knowing is about relationship rather than intellectual capacity. Truly knowing another does not mean you know every thought or understand every decision, but that you are held in relationship, knowing what has been revealed. God has revealed Himself to us through His Word and the Word made flesh—His Son—and this knowledge is the fullness of what He intended to reveal. He has hidden nothing from us that must be known to trust Him. His revelation is sufficient for our salvation. He cannot be known fully, but He can be known truly. And what we know truly is that there is nothing that is not good about God lurking in darkness. Even what we do not know is good.

While we only see dimly, just a shadow of His true light, we know enough to know Him truly because when we look at Jesus, we see God. Not like when we look at a child, we see their father's eyes and their mother's smile. When we look at Jesus, we see God because He is God, and we see Him clearly in the pages of Scripture. While we await the day we'll see Him face-to-face, Scripture tells us what we need to know to believe and to know Him rightly, and one day we will comprehend Him fully.

We cannot fully comprehend the brilliance of the sun because to gaze upon it too long will cause our eyes to ache from its radiance. We don't know everything there is to know about the sun, but we still feel the warmth of its light on our face. While I haven't comprehended the implications of Einstein's theories, I understand that they are scientific marvels. While I do not yet comprehend the German language, I know that it is the language of many, and I often recognize its cadence and impressively aggressive articulation. I cannot comprehend the circumference of the world because I haven't experienced it in its fullness, but I know that it is 24,901 miles. I can't comprehend these things, but I know them. I cannot get my mind around the fullness of God, but I can know Him.

This is our best news, our only boast-worthy truth. It is better than wisdom, strength, or wealth, because in knowing God, we get to participate in life with Him—this abundant, miraculous, full-of-joy life that is only available to those who are in Christ because we know Him. How are you seeking to grow in that knowledge today?

> "This is eternal life: that they may know you, the only true God,
> and the one you have sent—Jesus Christ." (John 17:3)

ADDITIONAL READING: Proverbs 8:17; 1 Corinthians 2:9–10; 2 Peter 3:18

COMING HOME

*For this is what the L*ORD *says: "When seventy years for Babylon are complete, I will attend to you and will confirm my promise concerning you to restore you to this place. For I know the plans I have for you"—this is the L*ORD'*s declaration—"plans for your well-being, not for disaster, to give you a future and a hope. You will call to me and come and pray to me, and I will listen to you. You will seek me and find me when you search for me with all your heart. I will be found by you"—this is the L*ORD'*s declaration—"and I will restore your fortunes and gather you from all the nations and places where I banished you"—this is the L*ORD'*s declaration. "I will restore you to the place from which I deported you."*
Jeremiah 29:10–14

Exile is the unifying theme of the history of God's people. Sin separated Adam and Eve from God, banishing them from the garden and sending them out into a land they did not know and which was not the good land of God's promise. They were no longer under the great shade of God's righteous outstretched hand, but were sent into a harsher land with little hope of return. The thorns and thistles grew, and the sweat wiped from their brows came through difficulty and pain, exiled from the good life in God's presence and enslaved by sin in a place that was not their intended home. They were exiled both physically and spiritually, a pattern that persisted until the Son chose to exile Himself into a fallen world so that He might not just be with His people, but so He could bring them back from exile into the presence of God.

Adam and Eve are exiled from the garden and then, shortly after, Cain's sin exiles him even further into the wilderness. The Assyrians exiled God's people during King Ahaz's time, and the Babylonians exiled them during Daniel's time. And while being taken from your home and forced to live somewhere else under a different ruler is terror-inducing, the greater exile is that of our hearts. We are exiled by our own sin, often leaving the goodness of God on our own accord to pursue what we believe will be better—like sin will somehow lead to life and flourishing rather than death and decay. We subject ourselves to exile and then wonder how we got so far from home.

In the verses above, Jeremiah is writing to those who have experienced the Babylonian exile, taken from their homes and made to serve the will of another king. He encourages them in this same chapter to build houses and plant gardens, in effect saying, "Get comfortable with the discomfort, it is going to be a while." Seventy years of exile would pass in Babylon before God would miraculously bring them back into the Promised Land. Seventy years. An entire generation would live in exile, many only able to imagine the land their hearts yearned for because they had never seen it.

While God was the one who banished them there (v. 14) by orchestrating the actions of Babylon, He would also be the One who would bring them home. His plans are good for His people, even if struggle continues for seven decades. They are good, even for those whose eyes will never open in the Promised Land again. They are good not because the situations are good, but because God is good and no matter what we face in this incredibly broken world, He faces it with us. God doesn't call evil good, but He does walk it with us, allowing us to see His goodness, even in our great suffering.

God calls His people to seek Him and call out to Him. Before they could return to their land they needed to return to their God. Before they could experience His blessing, they needed to experience His favor. God called them to seek Him, not His kindness. Seek Him, not His favor. Seek the One who had brought them out of Egypt and out of the hands of the Assyrians. The One who had fought for them time and time again. He would bring them back.

The Son willingly chose to take on flesh, leaving the divine fellowship and comfort of the Godhead. While present in and with Him, He left heaven to be united with broken flesh—those who He dearly loved but who were exiled from communion with God. When we couldn't find our way back to God on our own, Jesus came not to show us the way, but to *be* the Way. When we couldn't ascend to God, He descended to us, making us able to ascend with Him to the heavenly places not because we are suddenly able ourselves, but because we are hidden within Him and He is able.

God's promise is not just for the exiles of Babylon. This world is not our home, but we might as well build some gardens while we await Jesus's return to finish the task of bringing us home. He won't only bring us home from exile, but He has built us a home. He won't just allow us to be in His presence, but to enjoy it. And we will dwell in the house of the Lord forever (Ps. 23:6).

ADDITIONAL READING: Jeremiah 24:7; Hosea 6:1; Zechariah 1:3; James 4:8

BEGINNING AND END

*"I am the Alpha and the Omega," says the Lord God, "the
one who is, who was, and who is to come, the Almighty."*
Revelation 1:8

Before the starting gun sounds, the crowd of runners looks like they've
stirred up an ant bed. They shake out their arms and legs, finding an
outlet for the anxiety that is building. Toes get near the starting line as they
assume a ready-to-run position with their finger at their wrist, prepared to
start their smart watches as soon as the starting gun sounds.

The race clearly begins with a loud pop and ends when the last runner
crosses the finish line, long after the fastest runner powered through the ribbon that once hung there. What's in-between is a delicate balance between
pacing yourself and an all-out sprint.

First Corinthians equates our lives with a race, a moment in space and
time with a clear beginning and end, and with instructions to run as to
win. This is our mindset for all of life too, because not one earthly thing is
immune to this truth: everything we know that has an earthbound existence
has a beginning and an end, a birth and a death. As God the Son took on
flesh, He willingly embraced both by taking on humanity, but in His deity,

He had neither. God has no start or finish line, no clear boundary within time and space. Space and time are human dimensions that do not hold the Divine. Instead, the Divine holds both space and time in His hands, able to do as He pleases with it.

Instead, He is Alpha and Omega—the first and last letter of the Greek alphabet—Beginning and End. He is not held by time and space, but holds it in Himself. There has never been a time when God was not, when He was not God or when He was not sovereignly ruling over all. He has no beginning or end, but He *is* the Beginning and End, both Alpha and Omega, the first and last letter of the Greek alphabet. Tertullian says, ". . . just as Alpha rolls on till it reaches Omega, and again Omega rolls back till it reaches Alpha, in the same way He might show that in Himself is both the downward course of the beginning on to the end, and the backward course of the end up to the beginning; so that every economy, ending in Him through whom it began. . . ."[56]

He is the beginning of all things, the Sustainer of all things, and the ultimate end of all things. What peace this brings! The trustworthy, always faithful One is both beginning and end, and back to the beginning, and He cares for you—not just generally, but specifically. He sustains you specifically. He is at work in, through, for, and around you. He is not only innately involved in all the happenings of the world, He is the author. He has not joined in the middle, trying to figure out how to engage from here. He is not tossed to and fro by the winds of change and the fast-moving current of our lives. He is Lord of wind and water, knowing their every motion and commanding their sway.

He is not bound by time, unlike humanity that is enslaved to it, unable to add a moment more to our lives or to slow the setting sun to grant us just a few more minutes in a day. There is nothing that is not under His direction, from A to Z. Like a grand play director or the maestro of a symphony, God is producing the story of history, marching toward a rather than and known, clear end: the fullness of His glory in His dwelling with His people. He is all-powerful—Almighty—and He has been, is, and will be infinitely victorious in every way.

All of His attributes are outside of time, never changing. Augustine says it this way in *Confessions*:

> For you [God] are infinite and never change. In you "today" never comes to an end: and yet our "today" does come to an end in you, because time, as well as everything else, exists in you. If it did not, it would have no means of passing. And since your years never come to an end, for you they are simply "today" . . . But you yourself are eternally the same. In your "today" you will make all that is to exist tomorrow and thereafter, and in your "today" you have made all that existed yesterday and for ever before."[57]

This is our God. The One in whom and through whom all exists. He is the Alpha and the Omega, the Beginning and End. We highlight the cross as the moment in time that God worked out our salvation, but this does not mean this was the only time He was working out our salvation. Hebrews 4:3, says: "his works have been finished since the foundation of the world." Any who were found faithful before Jesus died on the cross weren't trusting in some hopeful perception of a Savior who might come, but in the One whose work is both in a specific moment and also before the foundations of the world. This is a great mystery, but what we do know is that the Son has always been and will always be God's Sent One, securing our salvation by taking on our broken humanity and healing it from the inside out. He is the Alpha and Omega, infinite in every direction, and this infinitude is in all good things: life and light, love and grace.

You are in a race. You may be at the starting line, still shaking out the jitters; or you may be thirty yards from the ribbon, sprinting harder than you've ever sprinted before; or you may be walking or dancing along, pretending like there's no real race at all. Remember to run in such a way as to win the prize (1 Cor. 9:24–27). The finish line is closer every day on this race that Christ has already won on our behalf. In His goodness, the finish ribbon has already been crossed, and for anyone in Christ, they've been declared victorious. Run as those who've tasted and seen that the Lord is good—that He has already finished the work of your salvation and awaits the day that the fullness of its completion will be fulfilled. He's coming soon.

> "Look, I am coming soon, and my reward is with me to repay each person according to his work. I am the Alpha and the Omega, the first and the last, the beginning and the end." (Rev. 22:12–13)

ADDITIONAL READING: Isaiah 44:6; Revelation 1:17–18; Revelation 21:6–7

GOD IS GOOD AND HE IS GOOD TO ME

"Who among you, if his son asks him for bread, will give him a stone? Or if he asks for a fish, will give him a snake? If you then, who are evil, know how to give good gifts to your children, how much more will your Father in heaven give good things to those who ask him."
Matthew 7:9–11

God punctuated each day of creation with the declaration of its goodness, a truth that could only be true if He Himself is the pinnacle of goodness. He has shared His goodness with all that He made, and even sin could not remove it. The earth reverberates with it: the brightest sunlight that is necessary for crops to grow and life-sustaining warmth, the separation of day and night so that our bodies know when to rest and when to wake, the water cycle, the food chain, the nitrogen cycle. All of earth sits in the balance of complex interrelated systems, each one of them flowing out of His goodness for our good. All He created is good and all He does is good. Creation is just the start. His redemption is good. His grace is good. His sharing of His attributes with us is good. His revelation of Himself in the Word and through Jesus is good. He is so good that the word *good* doesn't seem good enough to describe Him. He's not "good" like the half-hearted answer to How are you doing? or to "How was your day?" He is truly good, the perfection of His nature.

Though we are just children, immature in our knowledge of what even to ask of God, He is a good Father, providing for our needs always in a way that is good. At times, we are given bread rather than the cake we desire, because good things aren't always the desired thing, but they are always the right thing. Over and over again, God does what is right for His people, even when they lived in utter disobedience.

He is the good thing, the highest good, the prize of salvation. He is the essence of good—its source, its standard, and its definition. He is morally excellent, perfect in all His ways, and He never fails. He knows how to give good gifts to His children because good gifts are all He has and all He is. It is like the warmth of the sun, wholly unavoidable, even if you choose to sit in the shade under the heaviest foliage cover. In the middle of the deepest rainforest, its dirt floor may be dark and cool, but it is never as dark or cold as it could be because of the sun's good heat that filters through the leaves. It is possible to keep our heads down as we walk amongst the dense foliage, ignoring the sun with no awareness, that just beyond the limbs and leaves, the glory of the sun shines brightly. In our lives, this looks like turning our back on God's good to choose a path of our own, one we believe will be better than His good. We often have to experience the dissatisfaction and frustration that comes with going our own way before we see clearly the goodness of our Father. He truly is our highest good. There is no better life without Him—in fact, there is no true life without Him. Every goodness we experience is from His hand. Every goodness is an overflow of His nature.

In a world of difficulty, His goodness sustains us. The greatest outworking of this goodness is the One who took on our broken flesh, healing it from the inside out. He is the One who hung on a tree, cursed (Gal. 3:13), reversing the curse that came from the tree of the knowledge of good and evil. This is why we can take on the perspective of Job when dark clouds come our way. Job, who lost more than I can imagine by no fault of his own, cried out what I hope will be true of us: "Though he slay me, I will hope in him . . ." (Job 13:15 ESV). Though He slay me, I trust His goodness.

While the world quakes beneath our feet and the trials often seem crushing, His goodness is constant. It is infinite. It is for all the world, but it also is for you. He is good, but He is also good to you. To me. His goodness never fails. As Martin Luther says, "This is true faith, a living confidence in the goodness of God."[58] This is faith: to know the Goodness of God, who is Christ. This is the One we worship, the One who is good. May we be changed by His goodness and overwhelmed by His grace. May we trust Him more because we have seen His "goodness in the land of the living" (Ps. 27:13) and have found Him to be better than anything this world has to offer. May we know Him, fully and truly, so that we may worship Him fully and truly.

ADDITIONAL READING: Ezra 3:11; Psalm 143:10; Matthew 7:11; Luke 12:27–34

EPILOGUE

One hundred entries would never be enough to proclaim God's goodness in its fullness, but I pray that you've seen Him clearly in these pages. He is our highest good, the prize of our salvation. Communion with Him is the glory of the Christian life, the gift of an eternity of knowing and loving Him as He knows and loves you. This is a lifelong journey, a never-ending joy of discovering more and more. I'm praying that as you close this book, you are committed to a lifetime in His Word. May God use it to change you and cultivate good fruit in you from the inside out.

Who else can you take with you? The goodness of God is too wonderful to keep to yourself. Let's fix our eyes on God who is our highest good . . . together.

ABOUT THE AUTHOR

Mary Wiley is an author, Bible teacher, and publisher, working on resources everyday that help readers better understand God's Word. She is the author of *Everyday Theology*, an eight-week Bible study exploring essential doctrines and why they matter in our everyday lives. She holds a BA in Christian studies and English from the University of Mobile and an MA in theological studies from The Southern Baptist Theological Seminary. She and her husband, John, have three children and live in the Nashville area. You can follow her @marycwiley.

NOTES

1. Dorothy L. Sayers, *The Whimsical Christian: 18 Essays* (New York: Collier Books, 1987), 27–28.

2. *Merriam-Webster.com Dictionary*, s.v. "summum bonum," https://www.merriam-webster.com/dictionary/summum%20bonum. Accessed August 10, 2023.

3. Herman Bavinck, *Our Reasonable Faith* (Grand Rapids: W. B. Eerdmans, 1956).

4. This language is Dr. Gregg Allison's, mentioned in a conversation in January of 2023.

5. Drawn from *Saint Augustine: On Genesis* (New York: New York City Press, 2002) as recorded in Frances Young's *God's Presence* (Cambridge, UK: Cambridge University Press, 2013).

6. Ambrose of Milan, "Hexameron, Paradise, and Cain and Abel," *The Fathers of the Church: A New Translation*, vol. 42 (New York: Fathers of the Church, Inc., 1961), 347.

7. Victor P. Hamilton, *The Book of Genesis, Chapters 1–17*, The New International Commentary on the Old Testament (Grand Rapids: Wm. B. Eerdmans, 1990), 156.

8. Sigmund Mowinckel, "The Name of the God of Moses," *HUCA* 32 (1961): 127.

9. The Nicene Creed, Christian Classics Ethereal Library, https://www.ccel.org/creeds/nicene.creed.html. Accessed June 1, 2023.

10. Leo Sands, "How Often Do Men Think about Ancient Rome? Quite Frequently, It Seems," *Washington Post*, September 14, 2023, https://www.washingtonpost.com/lifestyle/2023/09/14/roman-empire-trend-men-tiktok/. Accessed October 1, 2023.

11. Andrew E. Hill and John H. Walton, *A Survey of the Old Testament* (Grand Rapids: Zondervan, 2009), 62–63, 112.

12. A. J. Wensinck, *Mystic Treatises by Isaac of Nineveh, translated from Bedjan's Syriac Text with an Introduction and Registers* (Amsterdam: Royal Academy of Science, 1923), 231.

13. W. Robertson Nicoll, Jane T. Stoddart, and James Moffatt, eds., *The Expositor's Dictionary of Texts: Genesis to St. Mark,* vol. 1 (New York: Hodder and Stoughton; George H. Doran Company, 1910), 140.

14. Adonis Vidu, *The Same God Who Works All Things* (Grand Rapids: Eerdmans, 2021), 59.

15. I. Mendelson, "Slavery in the Ancient Near East," *The Biblical Archaeologist*, Vol. 9, No. 4 (December 1946): 74–88, https://www-jstor-org.ezproxy.sebts.edu/stable/3209170?seq=1.

16. Elisabeth Elliot, *Suffering Is Never for Nothing* (Nashville: B&H Publishing Group, 2019).

17. A. W. Tozer, *The Attributes of God,* vol. 1 (Camp Hill, PA: Zur Ltd., 1997). As first recorded in Tozer's "The Omnipresence of God: Attributes of God Series 7 of 10," November 2, 1958, https://tozertalks.com/wp-content/uploads/2021/04/Tape-199Aa-11-2-1958-The-Omnipresence-of-God-Attributes-of-God-7-of-10-2.pdf.

18. This concept is gleaned from A. W. Tozer's *The Attributes of God, Volume 1: A Journey in the Father's Heart* (Camp Hill, PA: WingSpread Publishers, 2007). It is presented throughout this work.

19. Jennie Wilson, "Hold to God's Unchanging Hand." Public domain.

20. Helen Howarth Lemmel, "Turn Your Eyes Upon Jesus" also know as "The Heavenly Vision," *Glad* Songs (Elgin, IL: Brethren Publishing House, 1922). Public domain.

21. Story of Helen Lemell as seen in newspaper clippings like the *Shreveport Journal,* March 27, 1957, https://christianheritage.info/places/united-states/washington/seattle/organization-1/helen-lemmel-ballard-baptist-church/. Accessed September 4, 2023.

22. Helen Howarth Lemmel, "Turn Your Eyes Upon Jesus." Public domain.

23. Gregory of Nazianzus, *Letter 101, Epistola CI, To Presbyter Cledonius.* As translated at: https://earlychurchtexts.com/public/gregoryofnaz_critique_of_apolliniarianism.htm. Accessed September 4, 2023.

24. Arthur W. Pink, *The Attributes of God* (Auckland, New Zealand: The Floating Press, 2009), 49–56.

25. Michael Bird, "The 'Son of Man': Six Interesting Facts about a Disputed Title," New International Version, https://www.thenivbible.com/blog/the-son-of-man/. Accessed October 29, 2023.

26. Fred Zaspel, "Jesus Christ, the Son of Man," The Gospel Coalition, https://www.thegospelcoalition.org/essay/jesus-christ-son-man/#:~:text=Definition,most%20clearly%20at%20the%20cross. Accessed October 29, 2023.

27. Christine Comaford, "Got Inner Peace? 5 Ways to Get It NOW," *Forbes*, April 4, 2012, https://www.forbes.com/sites/christinecomaford/2012/04/04/got-inner-peace-5-ways-to-get-it-now/?sh=1c672d166672. Accessed October 1, 2023.

28. Katherine Sondregger, "The Humility of the Son of God," *Christology: Ancient and Modern*, eds. Oliver D. Crisp and Fred Sanders (Grand Rapids: Zondervan, 2013), 64.

29. Augustine, *City of God*, Book V.

30. Gregory of Nazianzus, *Epistle 101 to Cledonius the Priest Against Apollinarius*, https://www.newadvent.org/fathers/3103a.htm. Accessed July 8, 2023.

31. Saint Ignatius of Antioch, *First Epistle to the Ephesians*, Chapter VII, trans. by Alexander Roberts and James Donaldson, http://www.logoslibrary.org/ignatius/1ephesians1/07.html.

32. Andrew Murray, *Humility* (Nashville: B&H Publishing Group, 2017), 23.

33. https://www.plough.com/en/topics/culture/holidays/christmas-readings/mary-consoles-eve

34. Hannah Holbert, "Marriage in Ancient Mesopotamia and Babylonia," 2023, https://ehistory.osu.edu/articles/marriage-ancient-mesopotamia-and-babylonia#:~:text=During%20the%20ceremony%20of%20betrothal,live%20remained%20the%20sole%20issue. Accessed October 1, 2023.

35. A. Stewart, "Customs on betrothal and marriage in the Old Testament," https://biblicalstudies.org.uk/pdf/cbrfj/27_27.pdf. Accessed September 1, 2023.

36. Irenaeus, *Against Heresies* IV:12:4.

37. Peter Stoner and Robert Newman, "Science Speaks," Online revised edition 2005, https://yearofourlord.org/1_bible_divinity_of_christ/ScienceSpeaks.pdf. Accessed September 4, 2023.

38. *Ignatius—Bishop of Antioch, Letter to Polycarp*, 3.2.

39. Ligonier Ministries, "Firstfruits and Pentecost," June 10, 2010, https://www.ligonier.org/learn/devotionals/firstfruits-and-pentecost. Accessed July 15, 2023.

40. Daniel J. Levitin, "Why It's So Hard to Pay Attention, Explained by Science," Fast Company, September 23, 2015, https://www.fastcompany.com/3051417/why-its-so-hard-to-pay-attention-explained-by-science. Accessed October 15, 2023.

41. Richard Alleyne, "Welcome to the Information Age—174 Newspapers a Day," *The Telegraph*, February 11, 2011, https://www.telegraph.co.uk/news/science/science-news/8316534/Welcome-to-the-information-age-174-newspapers-a-day.html. Accessed October 18, 2023.

42. Charles R. Chaffin, *Numb: How the Information Age Dulls Our Senses and How We Can Get Them Back* (New York: Wiley, 2021).

43. Charles Wesley, "O For a Thousand Tongues to Sing," *A Selection of Psalms and Hymns*, Ninth Edition (London: Orger and Meryon, 1843), 47.

44. Gregg Allison, *Historical Theology* (Grand Rapids: Zondervan Academic, 2011), 277.

45. Augustine, *The City of God* (New York: Francis Cardinal Spellman, 1950), 129.

46. Herman Bavinck, *The Doctrine of God* (Grand Rapids: Eerdmans, 1951), 144.

47. Ligonier Ministries, The State of Theology, https://thestateoftheology.com. 2022. Accessed October 15, 2023.

48. Basil, On the Holy Spirit, in *The Nicene and Post-Nicene Fathers*, ed. Philip Schaff and Henry Wace, vol. 8 (1895; reprint, Peabody, MA: Hendrickson, 1994), 35.

49. Abby Forton, "Hymnology: The Story Behind 'Amazing Grace,'" (Geneva College: June 22, 2021), https://www.geneva.edu/blog/uncategorized/hymnology-amazing-grace. Accessed October 10, 2023.

50. John Newton, "Amazing Grace." Ppublic domain.

51. John Calvin, *Institutes*, 1:11.45.

52. José Salvador Alvarenga, "Lost at Sea: The Man Who Vanished for 14 Months," *The Guardian*, November 7, 2015, https://www.theguardian.com/world/2015/nov/07/fisherman-lost-at-sea-436-days-book-extract. Accessed September 1, 2023.

53. Michael Reeves, *Delighting in the Trinity: An Introduction to the Christian Faith* (Downers Grove, IL: IVP Academic, 2012), 119.

54. Kenneth L. Barker, *Micah, Nahum, Habakkuk, Zephaniah*, vol. 20, The New American Commentary (Nashville: Broadman & Holman Publishers, 1999), 159.

55. Augustine, *Confessions* (New York: The Christian Literature Company, 1896), 113.

56. Nissan Mindel, "Hagar," Chabad.org, https://www.chabad.org/library/article_cdo/aid/112053/jewish/Hagar.htm. Accessed September 4, 2023.

57. Britannica, "The Indulgences Controversy of Martin Luther," https://www.britannica.com/biography/Martin-Luther/The-indulgences-controversy. Accessed October 15, 2023.

58. Martin Luther, *The Table Talk of Martin Luther*, translated and edited by William Hazlitt (London: George Bell & Sons, 1875), 19.

59. Alexander Roberts and James Robertson, eds., *Ante-Nicene, Fathers: Volume 4. Fathers of the Third Century:, Part Fourth; Minucius Felix; Commodian; Origen, Parts First and Second*, rev. A. Cleveland Coxe (New York: Christian Literature Publishing Co., 1885), https://oll.libertyfund.org/title/coxe-ante-nicene-fathers-volume-4?html=trueTertullian.

60. Augustine, *Confessions*, Book I, Section 6.

61. *The Complete Works of Martin Luther*, vol. 2. Sermons 13–41.

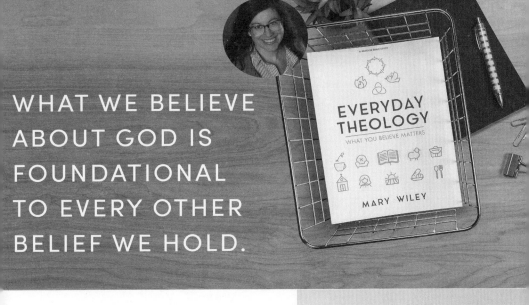

WHAT WE BELIEVE ABOUT GOD IS FOUNDATIONAL TO EVERY OTHER BELIEF WE HOLD.

Theology is the study of God, what He has done, is doing, and will do in the world. And it's not just for those with formal education or those who work at your church. It's for you in your everyday moments, questions, and decisions. It's for the big and little, the exciting and mundane. Our theology is the basis of our faith and touches every part of our existence.

In this 8-session study by Mary Wiley, explore the following essential doctrines: Scripture, God, Jesus, the Holy Spirit, humanity, redemption, the church, and the end times. Know God more deeply as you examine these foundational truths.

Available wherever books are sold.

 women